Strange Haven

Strange Haven

A Jewish Childhood in Wartime Shanghai

SIGMUND TOBIAS

FOREWORD BY MICHAEL BERENBAUM

UNIVERSITY OF ILLINOIS PRESS   URBANA AND CHICAGO

Publication of this book was supported by
the Sheldon Drobny Family Endowment
for the University of Illinois Press

The Library of Congress cataloged the cloth edition as follows:
Tobias, Sigmund.
Strange haven : a Jewish childhood in wartime Shanghai / Sigmund
Tobias ; introduction by Michael Berenbaum.
p.   cm.
Includes index.
ISBN 0-252-02453-2 (cloth : acid-free paper)
1. Tobias, Sigmund. 2. Refugees, Jewish—China—Shanghai—
Biography. 3. Jews, German—China—Shanghai—Biography.
I. Title.
DS135.C5 T63   1999
951'.13205'092—ddc21
[B]
98-25368
CIP

Paperback ISBN 978-0-252-07624-4

*I*n this book I describe a relatively obscure detail of the tragedy that was the Holocaust. I hope that my children, Susan and Rochelle Tobias, and grandchildren, Daniel and Jessica Schapiro, and their descendants will know and have a permanent record of one part of our family's history. I want to thank my wife, Lora, for acting as a patient, sensitive, helpful, and conscientious first reviewer on all the drafts of this manuscript.

This book was written to honor the memory of my parents, Frieda and Moses Tobias, whose courage gave continued life to our family.

Contents

Illustrations follow pages 74 and 146.

Foreword

MICHAEL BERENBAUM

I first met Sigmund Tobias almost thirty years ago when I was a young graduate student in Tallahassee. Although it is the capital of Florida and the home of a large university, Tallahassee at that time was culturally more southern Georgia than northern Florida, a very strange place indeed for a graduate of New York Yeshivot, a long-haired and bearded ordained rabbi. The only synagogue in town was Reform. The service was stately and formal, with prayers mostly in English—not quite the place I wanted to be for the high holidays. As a child of the sixties, I wanted more spirituality, greater informality, and more Yiddishkeit, an ethnic spirituality appropriate to the Days of Awe. I read in the newspapers about a group of young graduate students who were organizing traditional services for the holidays and joined the group. Over the next several months the group came together for prayer and study, for celebrations and fun. The high holidays were followed by camping on Succot, dancing on Simchat Torah, kindling the Chanukah light, reading the book of Esther on Purim, and observing the Passover seder. In early October Sig and Lora Tobias joined the group together with their then young daughters Susan and Rochelle. Sig—I don't ever recall hearing anyone call him Sigmund—was a professor, and we were then aspiring students. It quickly became apparent that Sig had a deep Jewish background and an intense Jewish commitment. The synagogue and its service were anything but strange to Sig, but still, as he entered its portals, one could feel the tensions, the sense of estrangement. Warmth, passion, deep Jewish roots, and equally deep Jewish knowledge were manifest in Sig, but so were alienation and discomfort.

As a group, we shared stories of our origins as we explored our Jewish roots. Fragments of Sig's story came out. Born in Germany, he was reared in Shanghai. He came to the United States on his own as a youth. Only later did his parents join him. Without a formal high school education, he entered college and went on to graduate school.

The professor had attended only three semesters of high school but had become a prominent researcher and an expert on test anxiety and school learning and on adapting instruction to student characteristics. He was also a trained psychologist and the only non-self-centered hedonist I have ever met. Having suffered enough, he was determined to enjoy life with a zest and a passion that were admirable and seemingly at odds with the heaviness of his experience and the depth of his commitment to education.

I had come to Tallahassee to study the theological implications of the Holocaust with Richard L. Rubenstein, who had only recently published his controversial book *After Auschwitz: Radical Theology and Contemporary Judaism,* in which he argued that after the murder of six million of our people Jews could no longer believe in the God of history. How could Jews believe that God was good, that God was just, that God was powerful, and that God was engaged in such a catastrophe? I had chosen Florida State University because Rubenstein alone was asking the questions that were becoming ever more central to my own evolving religious consciousness. Rubenstein was asking the questions that Sig Tobias had been living.

In discussions it became clear that Sig was reared an Orthodox Jew but could not reconcile the faith of his youth with the experience of his family, the murder of his people. Rubenstein was deeply influenced by Freud. So was Tobias, who associated religion with guilt. He had been made to feel guilty enough by his teachers in the yeshiva and by his parents.

That winter Lora's father died. Because she was far from family and friends, the community we had formed became a source of consolation to her. Her experience had been different than Sig's. Her family had lived in the same home in Schriesheim, Germany, for three hundred years until the Nazis came to power. Instead of finding a haven elsewhere first, she was the fortunate one who immigrated to the United States before the war, before the Holocaust.

Bits and pieces of Sig's story emerged, incongruous elements, but fragments of a whole. He was a Mirrer Yeshiva boy in Shanghai. Little did I know then, and perhaps little did he know then, the full story of the migration. The Mirrer Yeshiva had moved to Kovno, now Kaunas, Lithuania, after the German invasion of Poland in 1939. The students and scholars thought they would find safety in the independent state of Lithuania, only to be overwhelmed by the Red Army's invasion and endangered by the antireligious attitude of the Soviets. They searched desperately for safety and found an odd place of haven in a rather bizarre way. Chiune Sugihara, the Japanese consul-general in Kovno, had provided transit visas to Jews stranded in Kovno that allowed them to travel east via the Soviet Union and resettle in Shanghai. Among the people Sugihara rescued were yeshiva students, and the Mirrer Yeshiva was transported, students and teachers—even the library—from Lithuania and eventually ended up in China, where they all were safe and continued their studies uninterrupted throughout the war years. After the war the yeshiva students and teachers migrated to Brooklyn. The wandering Jews had gone from continent to continent until they found their freedom.

I was learning this information in 1972, at the very beginning of my formal studies of the Holocaust, a half dozen years before the docudrama *Holocaust* was aired on NBC, before the issue had traveled beyond the confines of the Jewish community, and before the heroes of the Holocaust—Schindler, Wallenberg, Zwartendyk, and Sugihara among them—were well known. Still, I knew that Sig had never been to Kovno, that he had not traveled with the Mirrer Yeshiva, but that he had arrived in Shanghai with his mother, two years prior to World War II.

Survivors were at that time still reluctant to speak; perhaps we, too, were reluctant to listen. I knew of Sig's somewhat difficult relationship with his parents. No one who has undergone psychoanalysis will fail to let slip some of what they learned on the couch, learned the hard way after much soul-searching. What I learned then from Sig was from the vantage point of a son seeking some distance from his parents, to differentiate and to distinguish, to establish a perspective on his world. Never did I hear of such an experience whole; perhaps Sig had never thought of it whole. Surely, he had not told it whole.

We did not then know much about the Jews in Shanghai, and the bits and pieces that we had heard were not part of a coherent picture. Quite frankly, it just didn't make sense. After all, Japan was a full partner in the Berlin-Rome Axis and was greatly influenced by Nazi propaganda. It had its own "experts" on Jewish affairs who wrote as well as translated anti-Semitic fliers that were subsidized by the German Foreign Ministry. Yet Japan also granted legal status to fifteen thousand stateless Russian Jews living in eight communities of northern Manchuria under Japanese control. Moreover, Japan provided a haven for seventeen thousand Jewish refugees from Germany, Austria, and Poland in Shanghai.

In 1939 Japan formulated a pro-Jewish policy enabling thousands of Jews to immigrate to the Japanese-occupied sector called Hongkew in Shanghai without visas or papers of any kind. It was virtually the only place in the world where Jews were welcome without visas. Sig and his family were the beneficiaries of that policy. In early 1941, when more than a thousand Polish Jewish refugees found themselves stranded in Kobe, Japan, with expired Japanese transit visas, the foreign minister of Japan, Yossuke Matsuoka, extended their visas and resettled them in Shanghai. The Japanese sensed a certain indebtedness to the Jews. The American Jewish banker Jacob Schiff had supported them financially during the 1905 war with Russia. Moreover, at a distance, the Japanese had mythologized the role of the Jews, exaggerating their influence and role in world history, an exaggeration that is maintained even into our era.

We did not know much of Sugihara either. Sugihara's role was, in fact, dependent on the work of the Dutch consul Jan Zwartendyk, who issued official-looking visas to Curacao, a Dutch colony in the Caribbean that required no visa. Armed with such a stamp, Chiune Sugihara actively assisted Jewish refugees in 1940 by giving them transit visas to cross Japan en route to Curacao and thus enabled Polish and Lithuanian Jews to travel through the Soviet Union and escape eastward. Three weeks before Soviet authorities intended to expel all foreign representatives, Sugihara granted transit visas to Polish Jews stranded in Kovno. For the next twenty-one days he devoted the bulk of his time to saving refugees. He said: "I cannot allow these people to die, people who had come to me with death staring them in the eyes. Whatever punishment may be imposed upon me, I know I should follow my conscience." By following his conscience more than seventeen hundred people were saved. He was honored by Israel as a righteous gentile years later. Yet for his efforts he was recalled back home and lived his life in disgrace for having misused the powers of his office.

But in this memoir the fragments come together so nicely. They weave into a tapestry that is whole, intense, passionate, and loving as Sig is intense, passionate, and loving. They benefit so much from the adult eye that Sig brings to his childhood experience.

Sig was born in 1932, the year before Adolph Hitler came to power, the last year that Jews could live freely in Germany. The child of Polish Jews, he was raised in Berlin and spent his childhood in an atmosphere that was internally loving and externally ever more dangerous. His recollections of Kristallnacht are instructive. The events of the November pogrom are well known. On the evening of November 9, 1938, anti-Jewish violence erupted throughout the Reich, which since March included Austria. The outburst appeared to be a spontaneous eruption of national anger at the assassination of a minor German embassy official in Paris by a seventeen-year-old Jewish youth, Herschel Grynszpan, himself the son of Polish Jews who had been expelled in October and forced to live in limbo between Poland and Germany. The violence, however, was choreographed in detail. Within forty-eight hours, 1,300 synagogues were burned, along with their Torah scrolls, Bibles, and prayer books; 30,000 Jews were arrested and sent to concentration camps; 7,000 businesses were smashed and looted; and 236 Jews were killed. Jewish cemeteries, hospitals, schools, and homes were destroyed. Jews learned that it was almost impossible to live as Jews in Germany. Sig's father, a stateless Jew, knew it was time to escape.

Germans, too, had learned important lessons. Urbanized Germans with bourgeois sensibilities opposed the events of Kristallnacht. The disorderliness of the pogroms and the explosive violence of the SA were soon replaced by the cold, calculated, disciplined, and controlled violence of the SS. They would dispose of the Jews out of the view of most Germans.

This is what historians know. It is ever more vivid when seen through the eyes of a six-year-old child: "We kept the curtains in our apartment drawn and used no lights to make it seem as if no one was home. . . . We spent most of that day and night in bed, getting up only when necessary. Kristallnacht passed slowly in darkness and in silence, interrupted only by our frightened reactions whenever the sounds of shattering glass made their way into our apartment from the street below." The child then went out with his parents and saw "charred handles of the holy Torah scrolls sticking out of the center of the simmering ashes." He recounts: "I had been taught to honor and respect the Torah. I had learned that the whole congregation would have to fast for forty days if the Torah was ever dropped, even by accident, during services. Now the Nazis had burned the Torahs as if they were nothing but trash. I suddenly knew that there was no safety for us anywhere." We do not know—and Sig cannot know—whether these were his recollections then or what he sensed as an adult recounting the story. After all, he has been on the couch, where he brought up many of these painful memories. He has returned to the past as an adult, with adult sensibilities and adult eyes. But still, there is a genuineness to his recollection. The adult memory contains the childhood fear. If Torahs can be burnt and people can parade around over those ashes, then there is no safety, at least not for those who bear the Torah.

In retrospect, the arrest of Sig's father, Moses Tobias, attempting to flee Germany in the post-Kristallnacht period, when Jews could surmise that things would only get worse, was the turning point in the saga of this one Jewish family. Before 1939 it was possible for Jews to leave a concentration camp if passage out of the country could be guaranteed. This chance for freedom might sound odd to nonhistorians or to casual readers who do not understand the evolution of the concentration camp and the development of German policy over time.

According to most historians, from 1933 onward until the winter of 1940–41 the goal of German policy was the forced emigration of Jews. The goal was to make Germany and German-held territories *Judenrein*, free of Jews. There were two obstacles to achieving this goal; both become evident in 1938.

There was no country that wanted to receive the Jews, at least not in the numbers that wanted to emigrate. And, more importantly, the German Reich kept expanding its territory, incorporating more and more Jews into its midst. Austria was incorporated in March 1938, Czechoslovakia shortly thereafter. By the end of September 1939 two million Jews of Poland, and in 1940, the Jews of western Europe, Holland and Denmark, Belgium and France, Luxembourg, Norway and Finland all came under German control. If emigration was conceivable in 1938, the sheer numbers involved made it a daunting task by 1940.

The political issues were unknown to the child, but not to his mother, Frieda. When Moses was captured, arrested, and sent to Dachau, his wife sprang into action. Unaware of the details, Sig could not know of the effort it took to discover that Shanghai was open to Jews and then to secure the funds for passage and make arrangements for that passage. Not a day could be wasted, for the opportunity to leave might be lost and, as a consequence, Moses would be condemned to life inside a concentration camp. Little did Frieda know that this sentence could become lethal, but she certainly intuited the danger and, hence, the immediate need to respond. Sig recalls what a child would actually remember. His father, a giant of a man, returned home beaten, broken, humbled: "Before everything became so frightening in Germany, I used to feel that my father could protect me from anything. After Dachau I saw that he could hardly take care of himself. During his last two days in Berlin before leaving for Shanghai I was scared when I looked at my father and ashamed when he caught my eyes jumping away from him." To the young boy, Moses seemed less large, less of a giant, less able to defend his family. Unable to protect himself, he could not provide security for his son. While for all boys the process of maturation reduces our fathers to size, it seldom happens to a six year old, and seldom so abruptly.

Flight was the response of the Tobias family, a response that was so very wise. It was not a difficult choice, it was the only choice. There was no nostalgia for Germany, and upon departure there was less a sense of loss than of relief. Historians often describe migration as a push-pull phenomenon. One feels a push to leave the land where one dwells and a pull to go to the country of migration. The push is obvious. They could not stay in Germany. The lure of Shanghai was equally clear. It was the only place they could go.

Life was difficult in Shanghai, but infinitely better than anything they had left behind. From lower-middle-class comfort the Tobias family was reduced to poverty, but not to starvation. There was always food, always something to eat, always shelter even when the Jewish community was ghettoized shortly after Pearl Harbor. Thus, even under terribly difficult conditions Moses Tobias was able to take care of his family, but under the Nazis the conditions of the Jews were far worse than merely "terribly difficult." Shanghai was a multiethnic city and the Japanese controlled the city's Chinese populations. There were elite Sephardic Jews from Iraq, Syria, and other parts of the Middle East who had long lived and prospered in Shanghai, as well as the new immigrants from Germany. They were later to be joined by Jews from Lithuania and Poland. The British ruled the International Settlement. The more comfortable Jews had built a community in Shanghai replete with synagogues and schools.

The life Sig describes is colorful, taking place in the outdoors because of the sweltering heat of the city in summertime. But Sig also describes the water that was unsafe to drink, the fresh vegetables that could not be eaten, and the constant struggles against bugs, the results of unsanitary conditions. It was paradise compared with the fate of the Jews that were left behind, but their fate was still unknown in the immigrant community.

Sig describes his school days at the Kadoorie school, where English was the language of instruction. His concerns are those of a young boy: acceptance by one's peers, performance at school, and the special attention that his tilted head called upon himself. The arrival of the Mirrer Yeshiva students brought the war in Europe home to the Jewish refugees, most of whom had left family and friends behind in their flight to freedom. With Japan's entry into World War II, the Japanese army marched in and took control of the International Settlement and French concession of the city. The British and the Americans disappeared from the streets, and the Japanese had more to worry about than these Jews.

An indifferent student, Sig flourished in his discussions with the yeshiva students. One senses that Sig was adopted by these boys and their teachers, relieved of the awkwardness that had characterized his stay in the less devout school. His parents, Orthodox Jews themselves, were not pleased with his newfound piety or his new friends. Yeshiva students, they reminded him, were the poorest students in Poland, forced to rely upon others for their survival. Still, with the scarcity of food during the war and the rationing of all supplies, the yeshiva students seemed better off, better fed. It was clear to Sig's parents that the yeshiva must have been receiving money from America. Sig joined the yeshiva, in part to alleviate his parents' deteriorating conditions. Throughout the war the Mirrer Yeshiva continued to function, providing for some 250–300 students who were taught in Shanghai much as they would have been taught in Poland, Lithuania, Palestine, or Brooklyn. Insulated from their environment, they were the epitome of inner-directed youth. For those unfamiliar with yeshiva education of the "old school," these chapters in Sig's memoir will have a charm of their own, even as the narrator is struck by the incongruity of his beliefs and education in the world of the Holocaust.

Throughout this period news of the war and the fate of the Jews trickled into Shanghai. One piece of bad news was followed by another. For Sig's parents this news was concrete—dangers faced by family and friends, silence from those with whom they were closest, fears, dread. There was no CNN and no sense of the accuracy of reports or even of the progress of the war, only deep concerns and even deeper fear. When the news became certain that the fate of those left behind was slaughter and death, Frieda grieved. To the newly pledged yeshiva student, this was a crisis of faith:

> One day she [Frieda] asked one of my teachers in the yeshiva, "If there is a God in heaven, how could he allow the most learned, the most religious part of the Jewish community to be slaughtered like that?"
>
> My teacher answered, "If you slap someone, you slap him in the face."

Frieda did not understand the answer and neither did Sig.

Sig had his bar mitzvah shortly after the war ended. As a yeshiva student he was well trained. Much was expected. Sig was to chant all of the Torah portion for that week, to give a speech, and to give a learned address. On the day of his bar mitzvah an American army officer, Rabbi Morris Gordon, happened upon the synagogue. He asked to speak to the congregation: "When I landed in Shanghai, I doubted if it would be possible to find a *minyan* (ten men needed for group prayer) for sabbath services. To my delight, not only do I find a vital synagogue here in Shanghai, but I am thrilled to participate in a bar mitzvah as deeply steeped in Jewish custom, learning, and values as one could ever have imagined anywhere on earth, much less in China. From this day on, the phrase *am yisroel chai* (the people of Israel live) will have a very special meaning to me for the rest of my life." Sig recalls there were few eyes free of tears, including "the American rabbi, my parents, and the bar mitzvah boy."

While I was reading Sig's memoir and listening to the more than four hours of tapes that he had made for the Survivors of the Shoah Visual History Foundation, my friend Rabbi Morris Gordon came to visit. As we sat in my office together with his wife, the eminent psychologist and educator Laurie Gordon, I quickly played Sig's tape, turning to the very moment where he mentions the visiting American rabbi. Morris recalled the speech verbatim. Fifty-two years after, he too could recite those lines. It was a tearful and joyful moment. Sig and Morris will speak before too long, they will share each other's tapes, and they will experience the fullness of the person behind the indelible memory.

After the war the questions for the Tobias family were where to go and how to get there. The yeshiva students were able to migrate to the United States, but Sig was left in limbo. He could not return to school so, as a fourteen year old, he began to work. As he entered the larger world he detected the anger of the community at the privileged status of the yeshiva boys. At fifteen he pressured his parents to permit him to travel to the United States, hoping that his parents would follow, which they did about a year later.

Less than sixteen, he set off for the abundance of America. Unlike most new immigrants, instead of going into business Sig, who had not completed elementary school and had barely attended high school, entered City College and later graduate school and became a prominent psychologist, educator, scholar, and author in a language he had learned in Shanghai. He never returned to the Mirrer Yeshiva except to visit its new quarters. "When I first walked into the building I had the strange feeling of being an outsider in the place that had been my second home for such a long time." The faith of his youth was lost. So, too, his innocence.

He leaves untold in this memoir his journey forth into America and the forty years between his departure from Shanghai and his return in 1988. As a scholar he was invited back to China to lecture and to teach in the very city he had lived in as a child. His trip back to Shanghai was warm and welcoming. It was the city that offered a haven to a very young boy and his family, the only place on earth where the Tobias family could feel welcome as Jews. Forty years later he revisited familiar sights. Little had changed in the landscape and the city, but so much had changed for the visitor. His heart was filled with gratitude. He remembered it all, but with less anguish and more warmth.

As for Sig today, after an impressive career at the City University of New York he serves as a Distinguished Scholar in the educational psychology program at Fordham University, one of America's leading Jesuit institutions. His expertise in test anxiety may have developed as a response to his poor performance at the Kadoorie school in Shanghai. His mind sharpened on Talmudic study, he later found school easy to master and could work as he studied.

You will read the story of one boy, a child lucky enough to have escaped, one so blessed in that cursed time. Sig well knows that he could have been one of the more than one million Jewish children who were murdered by the Nazis and their collaborators.

We have gained so much by Sig's life. Imagine what we lost from their deaths.

Preface

My parents were Polish Jews who decided to leave our home in Berlin after November 9, 1938. That date came to be known as Kristallnacht, the night of shattered glass that marked the beginning of the Holocaust. On Kristallnacht the German government incited the population to terrorize the country's Jews and vandalize their homes, businesses, and synagogues. After Kristallnacht my father realized that we had to leave Germany, thereby setting into motion our eventual escape to Shanghai.

Prior to the war many Jews wanted to flee from Germany but could not get visas to enter any other country in Europe or most other parts of the world. Surprisingly, however, visas were not needed to get into Hongkew, a section of the city of Shanghai in China ruled by the Japanese. Japan had been at war with China since 1936 and occupied Hongkew a year later.

Shanghai had a long history of foreign domination; two other parts of the city were ruled by Britain and France, and special privileges were extended to nine other countries—including Japan, which forced China to concede these areas in the middle of the nineteenth century. Shanghai's British International Settlement and the French concession were governed by the laws of these European countries, making it as difficult for refugees to disembark there as it was to enter those nations in Europe. Fortunately, the Japanese made it easy for us to settle in Hongkew. Our family, together with about seventeen thousand other European Jews, found a haven from the Holocaust. Beginning in December 1938 the refugees created an active community that continued to exist through the end of World War II and the early 1950s. No evidence of our lives there remained when I visited China forty years later to lecture at the Shanghai Institute of Education.

Shanghai, China's largest harbor city, was one of the world's more notorious pleasure capitals of that era. Few refugees could enjoy the available pleasures of this open city, having escaped from persecution in Nazi-dominated Europe with little more than their lives. Before the beginning of World War II European Jews streamed into Shanghai. Most came from Germany, with smaller groups originating in Austria, Poland, and other Eastern European countries. The final twelve hundred refugees arrived just before Japan's entry into World War II. This group consisted largely of a rabbinical seminary (yeshiva) from the Polish city of Mir that was renowned for its scholarly study of the Talmud (the authoritative Jewish law and lore). Eventually I studied in the Mirrer Yeshiva in Shanghai and spent my adolescence in one of the more infamous cities of the world as if I had been living in a shtetl.

The historian David Kranzler examined the files of the Japanese foreign service to produce *Japanese, Nazis, and Jews: The Jewish Refugee Community of Shanghai, 1938–1945*. Kranzler's book is a scholarly, informative, and readable historical account of our refugee community. Especially interesting was Kranzler's report of Japan's motivation for permitting the refugees to settle in Hongkew. Records of the Japanese foreign service indicated that before and during World War II the "Jewish problem" was being considered by a group of officers who had received their military training in prewar Germany, where they were indoctrinated with the standard anti-Semitic tracts used to incite the population against Jews. Many of these fictitious sources maintained that Jews were the world's foremost communists and financial manipulators.

Kranzler reported that an obscure historical detail reinforced the Japanese officers' beliefs about Jewish financial influence. Japan had fought and won a war against Russia in 1904–5. An American banker named Jacob Schiff tried to ameliorate the difficulties of his Russian

Jewish brethren by extending four loans to help finance Japanese expenditures during the war. In Japanese eyes Schiff's ability to put that financial package together lent credibility to the claims of worldwide Jewish financial influence.

Kranzler indicates that the Japanese officers tended to accept the Nazi propaganda that President Roosevelt was Jewish and actually named Rosenfeld. They believed that Jews controlled the United States (taking the fact that U.S. Treasury Secretary Henry Morgenthau was Jewish as confirmation for their theories). They theorized that if Japan treated the Jewish refugees well, then the Jews, who they believed controlled the United States, would make President Roosevelt more amenable toward Japan. They also hoped that American Jewish financiers would lend Japan money just as Schiff had. The officers also theorized that Jewish refugees might create a scientific and cultural class to settle in and develop Manchuria. Finally, in case the war with the United States went badly for Japan, reasonable treatment of the refugees in Shanghai might give them an avenue for rapprochement. Kranzler reports that in 1938 a Japanese emissary approached Rabbi Stephen Wise, a prominent American Jewish leader. The emissary told the rabbi that Japan had admitted Jews to Shanghai, an area under its control, when they were being turned away everywhere else in the world. The emissary suggested that this information should be brought to President Roosevelt's attention, but Rabbi Wise responded negatively to this idea.

Kranzler did a remarkable job of investigating the historical factors that led the Japanese to permit Jewish refugees to settle in Shanghai. Equally striking is Kranzler's feel for the Jewish ghetto community in one of China's most populous and most notorious cities, especially since he had never been there. Of course, Kranzler could not, nor did he intend to, give life to many of the people whom I remembered and especially to those who had not survived.

In this personal account I describe my memories of how our family got to China, our life there, the lives of our friends, and what we saw of the surrounding community. This book was stimulated by my return to China as a visiting professor at the Shanghai Institute of Education in 1988. During the four weeks of my return it often seemed as if I was walking through my past. Memories of our lives in Shanghai were refreshed by visits to our former homes and to other places that had been important to our community. These experiences gave me a chance to compare Shanghai after four decades with the city of a prior era.

To ensure the accuracy of my recollections I circulated a preliminary draft of this manuscript to twelve of my friends who had also been refugees in wartime Shanghai. I want to thank them for their corrections and suggestions, which I have incorporated. I am especially grateful to Norbert Seiden for an attentive reading of the draft. I also want to thank Walter Silberstein and Ruth Spiegler for their help with some details and Tom Oppenheimer for technical help in preparing photographs taken over fifty years ago for publication. The book also profited from suggestions made by Gary Porton and David Kranzler, and I appreciate their careful reading of the manuscript. Any remaining errors are, of course, my responsibility.

Strange Haven

1 Fleeing to Shanghai

*G*ray light was creeping through the curtains when I woke up, so daylight could not be far away. Very quietly, I slipped out of bed and tiptoed to our cabin's porthole. I looked for signs that we were finally approaching Shanghai but saw only the ocean waves advancing toward the ship. My movements woke my mother, who told me to go back to sleep because it would take at least four more hours before we reached Shanghai and caught sight of my father. Slowly I returned to bed and tried to fall asleep—but could not.

My mind raced over all the things that had happened to us during the last few months, jumping from one to another. Everything had changed, and all the changes were frightening. In Berlin a gang of teenage boys wearing the uniform of the Hitler Jugend (youth) often lay in wait for us after classes in the Ryke Strasse Synagogue School. Once we left the building they tried to corner us and would curse, kick, spit, and throw rocks or garbage. One day I made it part of the way home by myself when the gang suddenly appeared behind me. I fled, running as fast as my legs would carry me, but felt them gaining on me. I ran up to a very tall policeman, who looked mighty in his uniform and box-shaped hat while holding up his arm to stop a line of traffic. Panting and stuttering, I told the policeman that some kids were pursuing me and wanted to beat me up. He took a deep breath and seemed to get even taller as he said, "Well, we'll see about that!"

When the gang reached us the policeman was about to give them a good talking-to. Suddenly, one boy yelled out, "He's a Jew." Instantly, the policeman turned his back to me and went on directing traffic. I raced home and got there just before the gang caught up to me. I never went back to that school again.

Kristallnacht was even more frightening. We kept the curtains in our apartment drawn and used no lights to make it seem as if no one was home. My parents told me to be as quiet as possible; we tiptoed around the apartment in our socks, made do without running water, and did not use any knives, forks, or plates. My mother prepared enough sandwiches for the whole day and put them on the kitchen table along with cups of milk and water. When my mother brought me a sandwich, I forced myself to swallow a few bites. The finger in front of her pursed lips made it impossible to tell either of them that it hurt me to swallow because my throat was so dry. We spent most of that day and night in bed, getting up only when necessary. Kristallnacht passed slowly in darkness and in silence, interrupted only by our frightened reactions whenever the sounds of shattering glass made their way into our apartment from the street below.

After Kristallnacht had ended and it was safe to go out again, we finally left the apartment. I walked between my parents, clutching their hands. A Jewish family owned the grocery store near our house on Metzer Strasse. I often went there to pick up things for my parents. The store was empty now, its windows smashed and the shattered glass scattered all over the sidewalk in front of the shop. I turned my face away from the words *dirty Jew* that were splattered on the wall next to the store.

We walked away quickly and headed for the Ryke Strasse Synagogue. The temple was inside a large courtyard. When we passed the entrance to the synagogue that day, we saw a mountain of smoking ashes in the center of the courtyard. I saw that the mound consisted of burned prayer books and was terrified when I recognized the charred handles of the holy Torah scrolls sticking out of the center of the simmering ashes.

I had been taught to honor and respect the Torah. I had learned that the whole congregation would have to fast for forty days if the Torah was ever dropped, even by accident, during services. Now the Nazis had burned the Torahs as if they were nothing but trash. I suddenly knew that there was no safety for us anywhere.

I was glad when my parents decided to flee the country. My mother had kept her Polish citizenship when she arrived in Germany, and my name was added to her passport after I was born in 1932. With these papers we could get permission to leave Germany. My father had entered Germany from Poland without any papers when he was a young man and had been stateless ever since. No country gave visas to stateless Jews like my father, making it impossible for him to get out of Germany. A few weeks after Kristallnacht, just after my sixth birthday, my father joined a group of Jews who paid someone to smuggle them across the border into Belgium. My mother and I hoped to follow once my father had made his way safely to Antwerp. We spent many anxious days waiting for news of him. One day a printed postcard arrived stamped with a huge swastika; my father's name was typed into a blank space on the back. The card informed us that he was a prisoner in the Dachau concentration camp.

We learned that my father and his group had managed to cross the border into Belgium but had been caught by a Belgian patrol and turned over to the German police, who shipped them to the concentration camp. My father could be freed from Dachau only if he left Germany immediately. Of course, if he could have left Germany legally he would never have ended up in the concentration camp in the first place. My mother took me along to make the rounds of many consulates hoping to find someone who would give us a visa, even a temporary one, to get my father released from Dachau. We were refused everywhere.

In the waiting room of one consulate we overheard some people whispering that no visas were needed to enter the city of Shanghai in China. We had never heard of Shanghai before, but once my mother learned that the rumor was actually true she booked a passage on the next ship to China for my father. With ticket in hand she got him released from Dachau, and two days later my father left for Bremerhaven to board the ship for Shanghai.

My mother and I remained in Berlin for five more months. We felt isolated because all our relatives and friends had already left Germany. We went from one office to another to get the papers and tickets needed to join my father, give up our apartment, and sell what we could. We rented a furnished room for a few days, after moving from our apartment, to make the final arrangements for our voyage to China. One day my mother needed to take care of some details for our trip and asked me to remain in the furnished room by myself. She warned me to be very quiet and not to attract attention, especially by looking out of the window.

That day a parade was making its way down the street in front of the house. I remember peering at the marching bands in the procession through gaps in the closed venetian blinds. Suddenly, a German officer riding in an open car in the procession stood up and thrust his arm out rigidly in the Nazi salute while glancing up at my window. At that moment my heart missed a beat and I jumped into bed, pulling the covers over me. I could still hear the muffled band music and the sounds of marching boots pounding the pavement. When everything continued to be quiet in the house, I finally dared to stick my head out from under the covers and looked up. I was horrified to see the uniformed hats and rigidly raised arms of the marchers giving the Nazi salute bobbing across the room's ceiling.

I remember nothing else of that day until my mother returned. She told me that since it was a sunny day outside, the shadowy reflections of the marchers were probably thrown onto the ceiling from the windshields of the many cars in the parade. I took a deep breath when we finally left Berlin a few days later.

On the train to Genoa, where our ship would be docked, I slid into the furthest corner of the seats in our compartment and tried to shut out the sounds of shouted commands, thudding boots, and sliding doors being ripped open. When the noises were upon us the sliding door of our compartment was torn open by a uniformed officer shouting, *"Heil Hitler."* He ordered us to show our tickets and passport. My mother handed him the passport opened to the page showing the picture of both of us. The officer peered closely at her and then ordered me to step forward. I shrank from his look, with my face and eyes turned to the floor. He grabbed my arm, pulled me into the light, and pushed my chin up so that he could get a good look at my face. He stared at me, at the picture in the passport, and then back at me again. We held our breath until he shouted, *"Alles in ordnung"* (everything in order).

After he left my mother lifted me onto her lap without a word and held me tightly. As our journey continued, there were more inspections by other uniformed Germans and later by Italian officers in different uniforms and with softer voices. Finally, we arrived in Genoa and spent one night in a small room near the harbor before boarding the ship for Shanghai.

Everything changed the minute we stepped aboard the *Conte Biancamano.* A man in a white uniform with gold braids on both his hat and sleeves smiled when he took our tickets. He looked at them, bowed, and called another man over to help us. The second man speaking with the soft German accent of Italians said that he was our steward and would take care of us during the trip. He picked up our luggage and led the way through long corridors lined with doors, finally opening one of them and announcing that it was our cabin.

The brightly lit room was small, with two single beds and a porthole through which we could see the bustle on the dock. A bowl of fresh fruit was on a cabinet, next to some plates, knives, napkins, and a sparkling bottle of ice water with two shiny glasses. The steward asked if we would like something to eat or some milk or coffee, explaining that a snack would be served on deck once we left the harbor. Dinner would be later than usual on this first night of our voyage. My mother assured him that we did not need anything. He then offered to unpack our suitcases and left only after my mother thanked him, saying that we wanted to do that ourselves.

I was surprised at how nicely we were suddenly being treated and frightened that it might be some kind of trap. Noticing my worried expression, my mother explained that she had booked a first-class cabin for us because the cheaper cabins were sold out when she made our reservations. Waiting for less costly quarters would have kept us in Berlin even longer. We would be aboard ship for the next two weeks, and my mother told me to eat well and enjoy myself. Who knew what was waiting for us in China?

More food was served in the first-class dining room than I could possibly eat, but I tried to do as my mother had asked. I did not try many dishes that were strange to me, and we could not eat anything with meat because it was not kosher. My mother smiled when she saw me stuff myself with the wonderful breads, cheeses, fruits, and desserts. The weather was sunny and warm during most of our trip, and my mother seemed happy when my pale face started to tan a little after I spent most days sitting in comfortable chairs in the sun or exploring different parts of the ship.

Now that the last day of our voyage to Shanghai had finally arrived, my tossing and turning convinced my mother that we might as well get up. It was bright daylight when we stepped out on deck. I looked toward the front of the ship and, even though there was still no sign of land, wanted to stay on deck to search for the first glimpse of Shanghai. My mother made me follow her into the dining room to eat a hearty breakfast. It might be a long time, she told me for what must have been the hundredth time on this two-week voyage, before we would have so many different kinds of food again.

As the *Conte Biancamano* finally sailed into Shanghai and moved close to the dock, we strained to pick my father out of the waiting crowd. I worried about what he would look like now. Before Dachau I had always thought of my father as a giant. He was very tall and used to be quite strong. I was shocked at how much he had changed when he returned to Berlin after being in the concentration camp for only three weeks. He limped, dragged his left leg behind him, and seemed to have shrunk into his clothes. His face was ashen and his thick, bushy hair had been shaved off. After his release from Dachau it was hard for my father to pick me up. When he did manage to lift me, he quickly tried to sit down somewhere to shift my weight to his lap. Before everything became so frightening in Germany, I used to feel that my father could protect me from anything. After Dachau I saw that he could hardly take care of himself. During his last two days in Berlin before leaving for Shanghai I was scared when I looked at my father and ashamed when he caught my eyes jumping away from him.

Judging from the snapshots my father had sent from his five-week voyage around Africa to Shanghai he had gained some weight and appeared to have recovered from Dachau. But his hair was still very short and stubbly and had the look of the concentration camp. As I searched the crowd I worried about who would meet us now—my father or the man who had returned from Dachau.

It was easy to find my father in the waiting crowd; he was taller than many of the Europeans and towered above the Chinese. I was happy to see that his hair was as full and curly as it had always been. When we finally stepped ashore, I was relieved that he easily swept me up in his welcoming embrace. We all wept and held on to one another for a long time and did not pay much attention to what was happening around us.

After a while my father took charge of things. He found our luggage and brought four Chinese workers, he called them coolies, over to help us. I had noticed that the workers had been urging people to step into little carriages with one cushioned seat that were lined up near the dock. My father said that they were rickshaws and explained that the workers would take us to our house by running and pulling the rickshaws behind them. My mother and I got into the first rickshaw, our suitcases were loaded into the next two, and my father sat in the last one in order to keep an eye on everything.

As we left the dock I saw a soldier standing in a little hut; his right hand held a rifle with fixed bayonet that rested on the ground next to his feet. He was no taller than the Chinese people we had seen, but looked a little different from them. My mother said that he must be a Japanese soldier guarding the dock. She had explained to me on the ship that the Japanese had captured Hongkew, the part of Shanghai in which we would live, during the war between Japan and China that had started three years ago. The fighting was still going on in parts of China far from Shanghai. As the rickshaw runner went slowly through the streets, we saw that some buildings had been completely destroyed; piles of bricks littered the lots where people's homes and stores once had been. In other streets a standing wall or two, with holes where windows used to be, were all that remained of some buildings.

Even though it was early June the weather seemed much warmer than I ever remembered it being during summers in Berlin or on our visits to Poland. I began to feel sticky and uncomfortable pretty soon and started to squirm after sitting so close to my mother in the small rickshaw. The men ran slowly, pulling the shafts of the rickshaw through crowded and noisy streets, which were dirtier than any I had ever seen. They wore straw hats and were naked to the waist; their skin glistened as the sun picked up the sweat streaming off their faces and bodies. Gradually, dark stains appeared as the sweat dripped onto their pants, which were rolled up just above the knees. Strapped to their legs were rough rubber sandals that seemed to have been cut from truck tires.

On some street corners I saw small handcarts, some covered with huge dirty umbrellas. There were lots of pots and pans on the carts, and Chinese people were cooking on stoves set into the center of the carts. When the cooks were not busy stirring food in their pots, they fanned the coal stoves or their own sweaty faces. Some other Chinese people sat on narrow benches on one side of the carts. They lifted dishes to their lips and pushed food into their mouths with two thin sticks. My mother said that they were chopsticks and that these must be the street kitchens my father had written about. She was sure we would not be eating like that.

We soon pulled up in front of an open iron gate that was the entrance to a compound of houses. My father said that this was where we would live, the 737 Lane on Broadway, and that we were in house number 21. All the nearby houses had two stories and looked pretty much the same from the outside. The lane had a large main alley running down the middle; the entrances to houses were found in smaller alleys on both sides of the center; number 21 was the last house in the alley, right next to the rear wall of a warehouse that opened up onto the next street. My father used hand signs and a few Chinese words to direct the runners to take us to our house. When we got out of the rickshaw he told me to watch the other suitcases while he grabbed a couple of them and took my mother into the house. He soon came out again, motioned for the runners to pick up the remaining suitcases, and took me by the hand as we walked into the house.

On the second floor we stopped at an open door at the end of the hall. My father pointed to a sofa next to the wall at the front of the room, saying I would be sleeping there. There was a large wardrobe behind the couch and after that, at the rear of the room, were my parents' beds. An icebox, with a little drip pan underneath, stood on the other side of the room next to a dresser, and a small table with four chairs could be seen near the windows.

I used to think that we had a pretty small apartment in Berlin compared with those of our friends and relatives. I now saw that our three-
room apartment in Germany had been huge compared with our new
home in Shanghai. The one room in which the three of us would live
seemed only a little larger than our cabin on the *Conte Biancamano*. I
wondered how we would ever manage. There was only enough space
to unpack a few of our things; the rest stayed in the suitcases that my
father stored under the beds or piled on top of the wardrobe.

Later we met the seven other families also living in single rooms in
the house. I knew the Attermans, who had been our neighbors in
Berlin. My father had written from Shanghai that he and the Attermans were partners; they had taken out a long-term lease on a house
and were renting rooms to refugees. The other tenants had also fled
from Germany or Austria; many of their rooms were even smaller than
ours. At the head of the stairs was a kitchen, shared by the families
on the second floor, with a stove, some counters, and an iron sink.
Because there was no running hot water in the house, the sink had only
one faucet. The first floor had a similar kitchen, right next to the single bathroom used by all seven families in the house. The toilet cubi-
cle and shower stalls were made of rough concrete, giving them a dingy and unfinished appearance compared with our tiled bathroom in
Berlin. We learned that all the houses in the lane were similar to ours
and that about a third of them were homes to other refugees from
Europe.

It was not easy to get used to our new life in Shanghai. After a few
days I learned that our family was luckier than many other refugees
and almost all of the Chinese. A lot of refugees lived in tinier rooms
and in even more crowded houses, and some of their toilets, like those
of almost all the Chinese, didn't even have running water. We heard
that they had to make do with smelly buckets that were emptied by
Chinese workers every morning just before dawn. I was surprised to
see that many of the Chinese had these buckets right in their own
rooms.

During our first week in Shanghai my father took us to visit some of the Heime, group homes in which many poor refugee families lived. The people in the Heime ate in a common dining hall; my father explained that the refugee committee provided for them because they were too poor to buy their own food. In the Heime we saw huge rooms filled with wobbly steel double-decked beds whose lower and upper bunks were covered by thin mattresses. Often more than twenty people lived in these rooms. Sometimes only thin sheets or blankets hung over ropes tied to the walls separated the beds. After we visited the Heime our house on Broadway and our room did not feel so small.

2 Life in Shanghai's Lanes

After a few days in Shanghai I met some of the other Jewish kids living in our lane. They told me that a school had been started for the refugee children in Hongkew by Horace Kadoorie, a wealthy Jew from Iraq. It was now the second week of June, just before the beginning of the school's summer vacation. Since the next term would not start until September, there was no point in going to classes now. I spent most of that summer getting used to living in Shanghai.

A few Japanese civilians lived in our neighborhood, along with many Chinese people and some refugees. We had little contact with the Japanese and were glad that their soldiers left us alone most of the time. The Chinese were not so lucky. One day we walked down Broadway to visit the British-run International Settlement. We arrived at the Garden Bridge, the border between the Japanese zone and the International Settlement. A heavily armed Japanese soldier, with bayonet fixed to his rifle, stood guard on the middle of the bridge and was shouting at a Chinese man. Without any warning, the soldier stepped forward and smashed the man's head with the butt of the gun. I heard the heavy thud of the rifle against the Chinese man's head and saw him fall and begin to bleed heavily. The soldier kept kicking him and screaming until the beaten man crawled to safety.

I shrank back and grabbed my parents' hands as I pulled them away from the bridge. Even though the Japanese soldier was wearing khaki leggings that stretched from just below the knee down to his army shoes, in my mind's eye I saw the polished boots of a German Nazi soldier kicking the fallen man again and again. My father picked me up and explained that the Japanese soldiers often treated the Chinese roughly, but that they had nothing against Jews. The soldier would pay no attention to us, my father said, if we simply crossed the bridge and walked by without looking at him. My mother asked, "Isn't there another bridge we can use?"

As we walked toward the next bridge across the Soochow Creek that ran through the city my father tried to distract me. He pointed to the thousands of junks in the creek and to the people, including many children, who worked and lived on these long wooden boats loaded with different kinds of freight. The sails of the junks were dark and dirty; many were patched with stained brown and green materials covering holes that had been repaired again and again. When there was no breeze, the boats were moved along by straining Chinese workers shuffling along both sides of the junk and straining as they pushed against long bamboo poles dipped into the bottom of the creek. When the polers reached the end of the junk, they lifted the poles out of the water, trudged to the back of the boat, dipped the poles back into the water, and started their work all over again. Rivers of sweat poured down the polers' bodies as they gradually inched the junks through the muddy waters of the creek. The men sometimes groaned or hummed sad melodies as they kept at their work.

The people who worked on the boats also seemed to live on them. We could see pots, pans, dishes, and charcoal stoves in little huts on the decks. I was shocked to see people openly relieving themselves into the creek, while others lowered buckets from the junks to scoop up water for cooking and washing. My parents told me that our tap water came from the river and reminded me again, as they often had before, never to drink water unless I was sure that it had been boiled; we could not even eat the ices sold everywhere because they might have been made with impure water. We used no raw vegetables and ate only those fruits having thick skins, such as bananas. Most refugees were afraid they would catch cholera, typhoid, dysentery, or any of the other diseases we were learning about since arriving in Shanghai. Looking at the creek, it was easy to believe that we would get sick if we were not careful about what we ate and drank.

I took the fear of disease seriously. Chinese beggars roamed all over Shanghai; we could see groups of them on Broadway following the many foreigners who came to the docks only one block away from the street. The beggars showed off terrible sores on their bodies or stumps where arms or legs had been. When they were not following foreigners or well-dressed Chinese, the beggars sat on the sidewalk, propped up against a wall with flies buzzing all around them, and wailed their sad stories while waving a cup or a hat at anyone passing by. At first the beggars cried especially loudly when they saw any of the Jewish refugees, but they soon learned that we had little to give.

We spent most of the time during that summer in our lane, which was a busy place. Peddlers sold various wares throughout the day and announced their business with chants. Cars were forbidden in the lanes but tricycles, wheelbarrows, and other types of handcarts loaded with rice, vegetables, and fruits were pushed through the lanes. Other peddlers crammed their goods into baskets that were hanging from bamboo poles they carried over their shoulders. The poles were sharply bent from the heavy weight and seemed about to break at every step as the peddlers groaned from carrying such heavy loads.

Some peddlers pushed wheelbarrows loaded with big blocks of ice through the lanes, protecting them from the sun with layers of rags. They used picks to chip pieces off the huge block, sending slivers of ice flying through the air; Chinese kids often hung around the ice peddlers and eagerly scooped the slivers off the ground and popped them into their mouths before they melted in the heat. Other peddlers—some of them boys only a little older than me—sold ices in our lane and in the other streets of Shanghai. The ices were wrapped in a pile of thick and usually dirty rags and placed in a wooden box hanging from a strap carried around the peddler's shoulders. I often wondered why the ices were wrapped up like that, thinking that they would get really hot and melt in the heat of the day. A neighbor told me that the rags insulated the ices from the heat; if we had some insulation in our roof and walls, he explained, it would keep the heat away and make the houses feel a little cooler. Our neighbor warned that, because there was so little insulation, our house would also get very cold in the winter.

Barbers arrived in the lanes, each carrying a small wash basin in one hand, a stool and stand in the other, and a bag filled with tools slung over a shoulder. Once a barber found a customer and agreed on a price, he filled his basin with water from one of the houses and went to work right in the lane. Many Chinese men had all of their hair shaved off. The barber started cutting with scissors and hair clippers and then washed the remaining hair before shaving it off with a straight razor, stopping every now and then to sharpen the blade on a leather strap. When he finished, the hair-filled basins were poured onto the ground and the barber began looking for another customer.

Shoe repairmen also wandered through the lanes carrying sacks of tools. I watched curiously as one sat down on the ground and repaired all types of shoes right in the alley. He pulled hammers, nails, needles, scissors, heels, and many kinds of leather used for soles and shoe tops out of his sack as he needed them. A foot-shaped form made out of iron, on which the shoes were mounted during the repair, stood in the center of the stuff scattered all around the shoe repairman as he worked. New soles were cut from a big piece of leather that was rolled up in the bag and then hammered onto the shoe with nails the man kept between his lips. When the job was finished, all the tools and materials disappeared into the sack again, and the repairman went on his way. As they grew used to the refugees, the peddlers and workers wandering through the lanes picked up a few German words. It was funny to hear the Chinese shoe repairman chanting that he was a *Schuhmacher* (shoemaker in German) when he looked for work in our lane.

Keymakers also came into the lanes. Each pulled out a bunch of shiny uncut keys from his sack until he found the one needed. Then the edges of the key were ground with something that looked like a tiny sewing machine. A pedal spun a wheel attached to a metal grinder that cut edges into the new key. The workman then sharpened the key with different files and hammered it until the key fit the lock perfectly. My father never had keys made in the lane because he worried that the keymaker might run off another copy for himself or pass it on to others who would use it to rob our house while we were out.

On some streets letter writers worked at small tables and wrote Chinese characters onto flimsy sheets of paper using fine brushes; it seemed almost as if they painted each of the characters. Each customer sat on a stool next to the scribe and told him what to write and to whom the letter should be sent. The writer began by pouring a few drops of water onto a dark stone square; when enough water gathered, he stirred the liquid until it turned into a black ink. My father explained that the Chinese language was very complicated and that many Chinese people could not read or write. Customers paid the writers to prepare letters for their relatives.

Hongkew was also filled with shops, many different from anything we had ever seen. Some shops sold only herbs and Chinese medicines that hung in long strands in the store windows. Others dealt in incense; we bought some coil-shaped incense that was supposed to keep mosquitoes and other insects away. Once the coil was lit and placed under a table or chair, smoke began to curl up from the incense and spread around the area. We were told that the bugs could not stand the smoke, but it did not seem to chase very many of them away since

I was still bitten all the time. My mother never tired of warning me to stop scratching the bites all over my body.

There were also many pawn shops near our lane, and we were surprised to see European goods begin to show up in their windows. We guessed that some refugees needed money so badly that they had to pawn their belongings. Other stores sold coffins, and workers spent the day hammering wooden boards to make coffins of different sizes. The tiniest coffins were displayed in a window or in the front of the store. I did not need to ask anyone who would be buried in these small coffins.

Some shops in Hongkew sold heavy lacquer furniture or silk and brocades. Others dealt in beautiful fans made of ivory or of a fragrant wood. Many stores had lofts near the ceilings where bundles of folded bedding were stored during the daytime. After the shops closed, the workers could be seen squatting on the floors and eating their dinner. Later, they took the bedding from the lofts, spread the blankets on the floor, and went to sleep.

The Chinese bargained over the cost of everything. People haggled about the price of rickshaw rides and goods bought in the lanes or in the shops and markets. Even though we spoke very little Chinese, bargaining was surprisingly easy; we counted with fingers, showed money, and used lots of hand gestures. My parents were good at bargaining; they had been born in small towns in Poland where people also bargained. Also, as a textile peddler in Germany my father always bargained with his suppliers and his customers. Refugees who had never bargained before, especially those from Germany, had a hard time getting used to it. Even though I was born in Berlin I always thought of myself as a Polish Jew and joined my parents when they made fun of the German Jews for not realizing that they were being overcharged. My father taught me never to show too much interest in anything I wanted to buy, because it would drive up the price, and always to offer much less than was asked once the bargaining began.

It was also difficult to get used to the summer heat in Shanghai. By midafternoon the sun-baked pavement became soft and gooey enough to stick to the tires of cars and trucks; on the hottest days even bicycles and rickshaws left their tracks on the steaming streets. The intense humidity made the inside walls in our house so damp that drops of water sometimes actually dribbled down from the ceiling. We moved the sofa, beds, and furniture a few inches away from the walls so that our belongings would not get damp. I soon learned to stay away from the wet walls in our room because the water-based paint came off at the slightest touch, leaving finger or palm prints wherever we had made contact. At night the houses felt like ovens giving off the stored-up heat collected during the day. We all carried fans with us, but they helped only as long as we actually fanned ourselves, and we usually got tired of that pretty soon.

I was amazed to see Chinese women openly nursing their babies everywhere in Shanghai, not just in the lanes but even right out in the street. Although my mother repeatedly told me that it was wrong to look at them, I couldn't help staring when women unbuttoned their tunics and offered a breast to their infants while they shopped, talked to others, or went about their business. I could feel myself blushing as I stole glances at the women's breasts while trying to answer the many questions my mother kept asking me at those times. I soon learned that it was much easier to concentrate on the nursing women when I was alone.

I spent a lot of time watching one young woman in our lane. She often sat in the sun while nursing her young son, who could not have been more than two or three months old. She usually wore a T-shirt and pulled it up over both her breasts while her son was nursing, revealing her firm and shapely free breast with a large, erect nipple. One day she saw me staring at her out of our window and, while talking to another woman, tugged at her shirt until it covered her free breast completely. After that, I was careful to hide when I watched as she fed her son.

The lanes stayed busy all day and into the night. At the end of the steaming days people brought chairs into the alleys or out into the street to catch a breeze. Almost everyone tried to cool off by fanning their faces and bodies. During these long evenings the adults circulated the latest local rumors, discussed the events of the day, or examined over and over again the news from Europe. The most frightening topic was what might be happening to the relatives we had left behind.

We got most of our news from the *Shanghai Jewish Chronicle,* a refugee-run German-language daily newspaper. Isaac Atterman, our partner in the house, was one of the few refugees we knew who owned a radio. He and his son Willi were tailors and worked at home all day while listening to the radio tuned to European news or music. When a German news program was broadcast groups of refugees crowded around the Attermans' open windows to listen. Shanghai also had another German-language newspaper, the *East Asian Lloyd,* read mainly by non-Jewish Germans. We did not trust the *Lloyd* because it was usually filled with Nazi propaganda.

While the adults talked amongst themselves, I joined a group of three or four other boys. We tried to get as far away from our parents as possible. We played games and spent a lot of time trying to figure out exactly what was going on in the bar next to the entrance of our lane. Since Broadway was only a block from the docks, brightly lit bars lined the street. When foreign sailors on leave from their ships walked along the street, women waited outside and tried to lure them indoors. Most of the women working in the bars were Chinese, a few were Gypsies, and the largest group of foreign women was Russian. I learned that many of the Russians had come to China after their revolution. No refugee women worked in the bar next to our lane, but we heard rumors that some women from the Heime were seen in bars further down Broadway.

We overheard our parents and other adults say that these women earned money by dancing and drinking with the sailors. They received a share of what the sailors paid for drinks because they sipped tea or colored water, for which the customers were charged the price of liquor. Of course we soon figured out that the women were also paid for other favors. When it was time for those, the women and the sailors moved upstairs or to other private places that we had heard about but could not see.

On busy nights customers danced to the music of small bands in the bars along Broadway but made do with records or music from a radio on slower evenings. Swinging half-doors led into the bar next to our lane from the street. Although our parents did not allow us to hang around in front of the bar, we managed to find ways of getting there by picking up a ball or marble that just happened to roll until it came to rest right in front of the half-doors. We took our time searching for whatever we had schemed so hard to lose at just that spot and found it as slowly as possible. That gave us a few seconds to peek under the half-doors, take in some of what was happening in the bar, and report back to the rest of the boys. We saw a lot of dancing and some pretty heated necking. After that the women and sailors would move to places where we could not see them, although we certainly spent a lot of time imagining what must be going on.

Usually three or four women worked in the bar at one time, a Gypsy, a Russian, and one or two Chinese. They were always heavily made up, with dark eye shadow and deep red or scarlet lipstick. All the women wore tight, form-fitting, and revealing clothes; the tunics of the Chinese women were slit all the way up their legs, showing their thighs at every step. Bar girls often stepped through the swinging doors into the street to look for passing sailors. When I saw one of the bar girls during the day, I could not make up my mind whether to look at her or pretend not to see her at all. I usually got so flustered that I pretended not to see her. Of course, even then I watched her closely out of the corner of my eye.

Many stores on Broadway and its side streets seemed to sell nothing at all. These shops came to life in the late afternoon when Chinese women, as well as some Russian and Gypsy women, sat in the small front rooms when they weren't standing in the doorways trying to lure sailors inside. Most of the women chain-smoked, and some of them were dressed just like the bar girls. Whole streets near the docks appeared devoted to such stores, one right next to another. We pieced together scraps of overheard conversation and used our imagination to figure out what kind of business was being conducted in these shops.

Japanese soldiers often entered the bars and stores that contained only women. When the soldiers were not on duty, women were hanging around near them, and sometimes even some Chinese men. One day a handsome young Chinese man carrying packages of pictures wrapped in cellophane approached a group of Japanese soldiers standing in the street not far from our lane. A circle of soldiers quickly surrounded him and we soon heard gleeful laughter and good-natured cursing, while some money was changing hands. As the circle broke up, I saw the soldiers passing pictures back and forth. I tried hard to keep myself occupied nearby and managed to see that some of the snapshots showed young women who were partly or completely naked; other pictures showed the young man who had sold the photographs with the women.

Some of the older Chinese women had very tiny feet, not much larger than a baby's. I learned that the Chinese used to wrap bandages very tightly around the feet of young girls so that they would not grow too large. The Chinese considered big feet ugly, but that must have been true only for women's feet, because I never saw a man whose feet had been bound. It was easy to tell if a Chinese woman's feet had been bound when she was a child because she hobbled around in a stiff-legged walk. I often thought how uncomfortable it must be for a grown woman to balance herself on such tiny feet.

One evening I saw an older Chinese woman with those tiny feet hobbling along near our lane. A Japanese soldier, who must have been drunk because he was walking very unsteadily, was talking to the woman and pulling her roughly by her arms. I was shocked when, right there on the street, the soldier simply reached between the legs of the woman's pants. The old lady shook her head and pointed in the direction of one of the streets filled with stores empty of everything but women. The soldier turned and staggered off in that direction. The woman took a deep breath, pulled a rag out of a pocket in her pants, wiped her forehead with it, waited a few minutes to catch her breath, and hobbled off in another direction.

One hot day I noticed a rickshaw puller resting in front of our lane where the shadows of nearby houses provided some shelter from the broiling sun. The man sat on the floor of his rickshaw and seemed to be dozing while his head was propped against the seat. We often saw rickshaw runners resting like that during the hottest part of the day, when the streets were pretty empty. This man didn't move even when a Chinese woman hailed him. When she walked over to the rickshaw and prodded him with her foot, the man fell over sideways against the shafts of the rickshaw. Muttering to herself, the woman walked away and hailed another rickshaw.

I ran home to tell my parents what I had seen. When my father came back with me to take a look, he quickly shooed me home and agreed with my guess that the man had died.

"Shouldn't we do something?"

My father said that there was nothing to be done. When he first arrived in Shanghai the refugees reported the dead bodies to the police. The corpses were then collected, and those who made the report had to pay for the pickup. Bodies were already regularly collected by the city twice a week. Corpses were not found on the streets every day, but we saw them pretty often, usually in vacant lots littered with garbage and the ruins of houses. None of the refugees ever set foot in those lots because we often saw Chinese men relieving themselves there.

The body of the dead runner lay in front of our lane for several days; the rickshaw disappeared later that afternoon. During the next few days, whenever I left the lane I took special care to make a big circle around the corpse. Even though I tried not to look in that direction, I couldn't avoid seeing the flies buzzing around the body or ignore the terrible smell.

3   Getting Used to Shanghai

Once we left Hongkew, the section of the city ruled by the Japanese, Shanghai looked very different. We noticed fewer signs of destruction as we approached Hongkew's border with the British-ruled International Settlement or while walking to the French concession next to the settlement that was even further away from Hongkew. The European-ruled parts of Shanghai had not been attacked by the Japanese, and we saw no bombed out buildings or lots littered with rubble there.

The largest and nicest shops, department stores, and hotels in Shanghai were in the foreign parts of the city, as were the offices of many international banks and other types of businesses. One of the nicer buildings in the International Settlement housed the YMCA. It was right across the street from the race course and had the only indoor swimming pool in Shanghai. We heard rumors that a large sign forbidding the Chinese to enter the YMCA used to be posted near the entrance. Hongkew's only outstanding building was the Broadway Mansion, an eighteen-floor apartment house that was the highest building in Shanghai. The mansion was directly across the Garden Bridge from the International Settlement. Other than that, there were no foreign clubs, banks, or modern office buildings in Hongkew. The International Settlement and the French concession also had the most modern movie theaters that showed recent foreign films. The three movie theaters in Hongkew ran much older films and it was always difficult to make out what the character were saying either because the films or the projectors were old.

There were many streetcars, buses, and electric trolleys in the foreign parts of Shanghai. The streetcars had two coaches and three classes. Foreigners usually rode first class, in the smallest compartment at the front of the streetcar. The second class, right behind the first, was used by both Chinese passengers and some foreigners. The third class was in a separate car hitched to the lead car; it was the cheapest and most crowded of the three classes and was used mainly by Chinese passengers. Hongkew had much less public transportation than the foreign sections of the city. A streetcar ran along Broadway in front of our lane and there were some bus lines. We rarely used public transportation because we did not leave Hongkew very often and the buses and trolleys did not help us get around in Hongkew very well. We usually walked in order to save money and rode a rickshaw for short distances only when it was too hot or inconvenient to walk.

Refugees who did use the streetcars mentioned watching their belongings carefully while traveling. Shanghai had many skillful pickpockets, and we heard of people finding that their wallets or money had been stolen right out of their pockets on the way to work. Stories were also told of refugees who had rested briefcases or pocketbooks next to them on the streetcar. They sometimes reached their offices only to find that the outside of the briefcases had been cut and all the contents emptied without them knowing anything about it.

Everyone in our house had some firsthand experience with Shanghai's skillful thieves. We frequently heard noises in the middle of the night that seemed to come from the warehouse next door to us and from our roof. No one could determine what caused the noises. One day I returned home to find a bunch of policemen and people from our house examining bales of textiles lying in the lane in front of our house. It turned out that thieves had been stealing the textiles from the warehouse next to us and storing them under our roof and then removed them when there were few people around to notice what was happening. None of us had ever seen any of the bales, even though the policemen said that a lot of textiles were missing from the warehouse.

The homes of most foreigners in Shanghai, and of a few of the wealthier refugees, were in the European-run parts of the city. Most of the British and many Americans lived in the International Settlement. It was easy to see that the British were in charge there because all the important police officers were British and many sergeants and some of the policemen came from India or other parts of the British Empire. The Indians were often tall, sometimes bearded, and looked huge in their starched British uniforms topped off with high turbans.

Most people in Hongkew lived in very simple two-story houses much like ours, while many of the buildings in the International Settlement and in the French concession were impressive with six or seven floors reached by elevators. We were never inside any of these houses because we did not know anyone there. Gossip among the refugees, and what we could see for ourselves, convinced us that these apartment houses were every bit as modern and comfortable as the nicest ones we knew in Europe. The families living in the International Settlement and in the French concession employed servants, and we could see them being driven around town in their own automobiles by Chinese chauffeurs. When their children were seen in the streets they were often accompanied by ammas, Chinese maids, or other servants. The most important difference between Hongkew and the European-ruled parts of Shanghai was that Japanese soldiers were never seen outside of Hongkew.

A small group of British settlers in Shanghai were Sephardic Jews who had come from Iraq, Syria, and other parts of the Middle East. Many Sephardic families were important merchants in the East and had come to Shanghai years earlier to establish business branches. A Sephardic family owned the Sassoon Hotel, one of the nicest in the city, on Nanking Road and the Bund, the busiest corner in the International Settlement. Horace Kadoorie, who founded the school for the refugee children in Hongkew, was also a Sephardic Jew. We heard a great deal about the Sephardic families but rarely saw them. Beth Aharon, in the area of the International Settlement close to the edge of Hongkew, was the synagogue for the Sephardic Jews. It was a big, beautiful building made of white stone and seemed larger than the small group of Sephardic Jews needed. There was also a Jewish school in the settlement that was attended by children of the Sephardic and Russian Jewish families, as well as by some of the wealthier refugees.

The French section of the city was next to the settlement, furthest away from Hongkew; all its major streets had French names. Police officers in the French concession wore the same uniforms and the stiff pillbox hats with small round brims worn by the army and police in France. The French Club, a social organization, had well-kept grounds that took up almost a square block near Avenue Joffre, the main street in the French concession.

Many of the Russian Jews in Shanghai lived in the French concession. They fled to China after the Russian Revolution and settled in Harbin and Tsingtao in addition to Shanghai. Although they lived in Hongkew when they first came to China, they moved into the French concession once they had become successful in business. Some of the shops on Avenue Joffre were owned by Russian Jews, and there was a Jewish Hospital on Rue Pichon, a few blocks from Avenue Joffre. A Russian Jew, Rabbi Meir Ashkenazi, was the chief rabbi of Shanghai. When we arrived in China the Russian Jews were constructing the new synagogue, an impressive building on the Rue Tenent de la Tour.

Passenger ships from Europe arriving in Shanghai usually brought more Jews fleeing from Germany or Austria. Since we lived only a block away from the harbor we heard the loud blasts of the ships' horns as they steamed down the river before tying up at the docks. Jews arriving in Hongkew, as we had, could simply step ashore because the Japanese did not ask for any papers. Refugees whose ships docked in the European sections of Shanghai were not as lucky as we had been, because the authorities usually would not let anyone ashore without British or French visas. Of course if they had visas they would have gone to Britain or France, not China. Refugees arriving in the International Settlement or the French concession had to hire Chinese junks to sail them and their belongings up the river to Hongkew, where the Japanese let them enter Shanghai. Others arriving in the European-run sections of the city were piled into trucks by the authorities and driven to Hongkew. Most of the refugees settled there with us, although some of the wealthier families managed to rent nice apartments in the International Settlement or in the French concession.

Toward the end of our first summer Shanghai was hit by a typhoon. This mighty thunderstorm brought sheets of rain for most of the day, combined with fierce lightning and heavy thunder that seemed to shake our house. More rain fell in a few hours than we had ever seen, and when the typhoon ended our lane was flooded with water, as were many other streets. My father told us that typhoons hit the city fairly often and usually flooded parts of Hongkew. My mother refused to let me out into the flooded streets because she was afraid that I might catch a disease from the waters. Junk and garbage that had been collecting in the streets floated past our house. It took a few days before our lane and the nearby streets dried out completely. The temperatures dropped during the typhoon but the humidity was so high that everything we touched felt wet.

We also learned to deal with more insects and flies than we had ever seen before. Cockroaches, flies, and mosquitoes were everywhere, and we often saw rats and mice around the house. My mother scrubbed and sprayed time and again to get rid of these pests, but they always returned in a day or two because they fed on the street refuse. The Chinese often threw leftover food and other garbage into the streets, and the food vendors and street kitchens all over Hongkew added to the garbage that the bugs and pests feasted on.

The garbage in our lane was gathered in a concrete bin that was supposed to be covered by a heavy metal lid. Since refuse was picked up only once or twice a week, the bin was always overflowing and the lid wide open, surrounded by swarms of flies and bugs. Some flies got so big and fat that we could actually hear them droning as they flew into our room. Fortunately, these ugly creatures flew so slowly that they were easy to avoid or kill with one of the flyswatters we kept at hand. Fly traps, gluey yellow strips on which flies got stuck, were seen hanging from ceilings all over Hongkew. My mother wanted to buy a fly trap, but that was not very practical because sooner or later the sticky stuff was sure to trap one of us as we moved about our small home.

The tap water was not safe to drink unless it was first boiled. Every house in our lane had one or two gas stoves, which made it simple to boil water but heated up the kitchen and surrounding area quite a bit. Most of the residents of Hongkew lived in houses without gas or electric ranges; these people had to heat everything on little charcoal stoves large enough for only one pot at a time. Because it took so long to bring water to a boil on these charcoal stoves, it was common to buy boiled water in stores in other parts of Hongkew.

On our first Saturday in Shanghai my father took us to the synagogue he had been attending since coming to China. Oihel Moshe, a large synagogue housed in a three-story building on Ward Road in Hongkew, had been built by the Russian Jews after they first settled in Shanghai. Oihel Moshe was about to be closed because few people remained to worship there, but Rabbi Ashkenazi arranged to keep it open after so many Jewish refugees began arriving. The only member of the Russian Jewish community still at the synagogue was Mr. Ovadia, its president. A Talmud Torah, where Jewish boys were taught to read Hebrew prayers four afternoons a week after school and on Sunday morning, met on the third floor of the building. The courtyard behind the synagogue housed a bakery in a one-story building. It was used for only a few weeks before Passover to bake matzos, the unleavened bread eaten by Jews during that holiday. My father had some experience with baking, since his family had owned a bakery in Poland, and helped to prepare the matzo before our first Passover in Shanghai.

On Fridays many Orthodox Jewish families brought the live chickens they had purchased for the sabbath to a hut in the courtyard next to the synagogue for the ritual slaughter required for the meat to be kosher. I often watched the European-trained *shochet* (ritual slaughterer) kill the chickens with the one cut of the knife permitted. He explained to me that if a second slice with the knife was needed to kill the chicken, the meat would not be kosher and could not be eaten by Orthodox Jews. Sometimes the chickens seemed to stay alive for a few seconds after the slaughter. I was shocked to see them thrashing in the *shochet*'s grasp after their throats were cut. It was especially awful when the chickens were lively enough to scurry around the yard for a few moments before collapsing.

At the end of the summer the time for the high holy days arrived. Refugees from Germany who were Conservative or Reform Jews had their own congregations, and other groups of Jews rented some of the movie theaters in Hongkew to hold services. During services on Rosh Hashanah (Jewish New Year) and Yom Kippur (the Day of Atonement) in Shanghai there was a great deal of anxiety in the synagogue. War had broken out in Europe and little mail from there was still arriving in Shanghai. Everyone was worried about what might have happened to family and friends in Europe. My father had one brother in Palestine, but all his other relatives and all my mother's relatives were in Poland. After we heard that the Germans had captured much of Poland, most of the people in the synagogue became extremely worried.

A few refugees still made their way to Shanghai after the outbreak of the war. These people could not come to China by ship anymore because the Suez Canal, through which the *Conte Biancamano* had sailed, was now closed. Shanghai could also be reached by sailing around Africa on a five-week voyage, like the one my father had taken from Bremerhaven. Since most of the ships in Europe were being used for the war, that route out of Europe was also largely closed. The refugees arriving now traveled from Germany to Russia, which was not at war, crossed Siberia by railroad, and then took a Japanese ship to Shanghai. Siegfried Loebel, who became my best friend, moved into our lane in 1940 after his family arrived in Shanghai by that route, and since Sigi's father had an Eastern European background—just like my parents—our parents also became close friends.

Some refugees shipped their possessions to Shanghai in huge wooden crates, called lifts. The Nazis allowed Jews leaving Germany to take only a little money out of Europe, but they could take all their used belongings with them. Those who had been well off in Germany packed whatever would fit into the lifts and brought them to Shanghai. The lifts were filled with bulky European furniture, lots of heavy European clothing, and all kinds of kitchenware for which the refugees now had very little use. Since no one had enough space to unpack most of what they brought with them the lifts were stored in warehouses, called *godowns* in Shanghai. Fortunately, we did not bring a lift and did not have to sell all the belongings stored there, nor did we have to pay storage fees for the lifts. My father started a stand in an open air street market on Kungping Road to sell merchandise he bought from Jewish refugees to Chinese or Japanese people living in Hongkew. The money he earned from that, and the rent paid by our tenants, helped us eke out a living.

All the refugee children started school again at the end of our first summer in Shanghai. A few attended Saint Francis Xavier, a school run by Catholic missionaries. Another small group went to the Shanghai Jewish School next to the Sephardic synagogue in the International

Settlement. That school had been founded by Russian and Sephardic Jews and was attended mainly by their children. Most of the other refugee children went to the Shanghai Jewish Youth Association school founded by Horace Kadoorie. Everyone called this school SJYA or the Kadoorie school. SJYA opened in a rented building on Kinchow Road in Hongkew. Later Kadoorie donated the money to build an attractive new school complex on Chauffong Road. It was a U-shaped one-story building with classrooms on both sides of a lawn. The two wings were connected by a large hall in the center with an attached kitchen. We used the hall for assemblies, school plays, and gymnastics. When the weather was good, we had our calisthenics and gym classes on the lawn in the center of the school, which was also used for our soccer games.

At the Kadoorie school all the classes were taught in English and we used the same books—the teachers called them readers—as students in England. My parents and I, and most of the Jews from Eastern Europe, talked to each other mainly in Yiddish and a little Polish; we spoke German to the refugees from Austria and Germany. Before school started we had picked up a few words of English from contacts with police officers and other officials in the International Settlement. Many Chinese talked to us in a mixture of a few words of English, some Chinese, and lots of gestures. I picked up English pretty easily, though I had a difficult time learning how to write it. Lucie Hartwich, a refugee who had been a teacher in Germany, was SJYA's principal; she was strict, and all the students tried to avoid being noticed by her. A few young Russian women taught at the Kadoorie school, but most of our teachers were Jewish refugees. Leo Meyer, our gym teacher, led us in general exercises and calisthenics and was also the school's soccer coach.

The refugees in Hongkew organized a soccer league. The teams played against one another every weekend during the fall and winter on the lawn at the Chauffong Road Heim, which had a regulation-size soccer field. The best players from the league also formed the Jewish Recreation Club, which competed against teams from all over

Shanghai in matches held at the race course in the International Settlement. Leo Meyer was known as the best soccer player among the refugees and was the star of the Jewish Recreation Club's soccer team.

We behaved ourselves during gym periods with Meyer because sooner or later the boys in the class would have to toss a medicine ball back and forth with him. Most of us would have been happy to skip that part of gym class because Meyer would really zip the heavy medicine ball to those boys who had acted up. We knew we were in trouble when his mouth jerked as he released the ball. Whenever I was singled out for one of these special tosses, the impact of the medicine ball on my stomach knocked the breath out of me, and I would stagger back a few yards after catching the ball. Of course I pretended that it was just a regular catch even though it took a while before my breathing returned to normal.

At the end of the school day at SJYA many of the other boys and I learned how to read Hebrew in the Talmud Torah at Oihel Moshe. The two classes meeting there were taught by Polish refugees. They spoke Yiddish during the lessons, just as we did at home. Although I would have preferred to go home and stay in our lane after finishing SJYA instead of being stuck in another school, I felt at home in the Talmud Torah and was a much better student there than at the Kadoorie school.

At SJYA the other kids sometimes taunted me because my head was usually tilted a bit to the left. My uncle had first noticed that in Poland during our last visit there. My mother needed surgery for a serious gallstone problem at that time, and since the tilting of my head was hardly noticeable and not dangerous, my parents wouldn't even think about having anything done about it when everything in Germany was so difficult and dangerous. As I got older the tilting of my head became more noticeable and, when there was no teacher around, the kids at the Kadoorie school often made fun of me and called me *Schiefkopf* (crooked head) when we had an argument. I never knew what to do about that. Sometimes I fought with those who made fun of me, but when they were much bigger than I there was nothing I could do but turn away so that no one could see the tears in my eyes. No one ever called me *Schiefkopf* in the Talmud Torah.

Just before our second summer in Shanghai we heard that a summer camp had been organized for some of the refugee kids outside of the city. My parents wanted me to go, feeling that it would be nice for me to get away from the hot, dirty city and from our one small room. My mother kept saying I was lucky to have the chance to be away in camp for two weeks. She insisted that I would enjoy the clean air, the grass and trees, and all the camp activities. I was happy enough to be out of school for the summer and would have liked to stay close to home, but soon found myself on a hot and uncomfortable bus headed for summer camp.

The camp consisted of a group of small houses, the leader called them barracks, with tin roofs and wire screens instead of windows. The barracks were arranged around a big grassy area. The leader ordered us out of the buses and, as our names were called out, assigned each of us to one of the barracks. The first thing I noticed when we marched into our barrack was a wooden rack with unusual notches in it along one of the walls. One boy said that the rack must have been used to store soldiers' rifles; he used a broom to show us how rifles would fit into the racks. Others guessed that the Japanese army had used the barracks before they were turned into our camp.

I felt a knot forming in my stomach when we arrived at the camp and started to feel miserable; I was actually sick a short time later. I knew that we were supposed to have fun in this camp, but that didn't stop me from being nervous and scared, without quite knowing what I was afraid of. That first night in camp, and on many nights after that, I woke soaked in sweat from nightmares. I could remember only bits and pieces of what I had dreamed, and those usually had to do with some things my father had told us about the Dachau concentration camp.

In addition to feeling nervous and frightened in camp, swarms of mosquitoes attacked my arms throughout the day. I also complained of being bitten at night; the people in charge kept telling me that couldn't be true because mosquitoes were kept out of the barracks by the wire screens. My mattress was changed after I found signs of bed-bugs on the sheet. Even though I was ordered not to, I couldn't keep from scratching the bites on my arms. Scratching only made me feel even worse, and I soon had sores all over my arms.

I was delighted when the camp leader finally decided to send me home toward the end of the first week. I was happy to get back to our house, but my parents were shocked to see the bites and sores cover-ing my arms from the elbows down to my hands. They immediately took me to one of the doctors in Hongkew, a refugee from Germany, who said that the sores might become infected. He warned me that the ointment he would put on my arms was likely to sting at first but the itching and soreness would get better afterward. I caught my breath from the stinging pain when the iodine covered my sores, but now that I was home that hardly bothered me, and the itching did improve. For the next week or so I proudly paraded up and down our lane showing off my arms, which the iodine had tinted a bright orange from wrists to elbows, almost as if they were badges.

Since many of my friends were still in camp, I was by myself quite often that summer and spent a lot of time reading. One day while my parents were away I grew tired of reading and was looking out of the window trying to find something to do. A small crowd of Chinese people was milling around in front of a house in the next alley. Some of the men were holding Chinese musical instruments, while others were talking quietly to one another and sometimes glancing at the house behind them. A small cart, which looked a little nicer than the ones used to carry goods through the lanes, was wheeled into the small front yard of the house in the next alley and disappeared from view.

Somebody came out of the house and spoke to the people hold-ing the musical instruments. They formed two rows and began to play a slow, sad melody. In a while the cart, surrounded by people, was wheeled back into the alley. Three Chinese people, dressed in white robes made of a rough fabric and wearing hats that looked a lot like brown paper bags, came out of the house. They were sobbing. A procession started, beginning with the men playing their instruments, followed by the cart, which was hidden from my view by the musicians, and ending with the other Chinese people who had been waiting in front of the house.

As the cart was pulled past my window, I could finally see it clearly. I was shocked to see a tiny coffin, just like those usually displayed in the windows of coffin makers' shops, and suddenly understood that I was watching the funeral of what must have been a very small child. It was a shock for me to realize that even though the Chinese looked so different from us, spoke a strange language, and had weird customs, the people walking behind the cart felt exactly what I would have. When I turned away from the window in embarrassment and caught sight of myself in our only mirror, I also realized that my tears were no different from theirs.

4   War

We were a little better off than many of the other Jewish refugees in Hongkew. My mother was able to bring what was left of our savings to Shanghai because the German government could not stop a Polish citizen from taking money out of Berlin. German Jews were not so lucky. They could take only a little expense money out of Germany and often arrived in Shanghai with little more than their lifts, if they were able to take anything at all out of Europe. After we had been in Shanghai for a while, my father realized that he could not earn enough to support us by selling the belongings of the refugees to the Chinese and Japanese. In partnership with the Neufelds, another refugee family, my parents decided to use the rest of our savings to lease a second house on Seward Road. We continued to live on Broadway, where the Attermans were our partners, and hoped that other arriving refugees would rent rooms in the other house. There were still three empty rooms in the Seward Road house, and after the start of the war in Europe few new refugees came to Shanghai. We and the Neufelds worried about being able to rent these empty rooms.

Much to our surprise almost 1,200 Jews from Poland suddenly turned up in Shanghai during the winter of 1941. The largest group of the new arrivals were part of the yeshiva (rabbinical seminary) originally from the Polish town of Mir. Students in the Mirrer Yeshiva were famous for their mastery of the Talmud. Most of the students were single young men, though a few families also accompanied them. In addition to the Mirrer Yeshiva, the new refugees also included two smaller groups of yeshiva students who originally came from the Polish towns of Lublin and Lubavitch. These groups were Chassidim, Orthodox Jews who felt a deep, personal relationship with God in their prayers, songs, and day-to-day life. Chassidim studied mystical writings and did not spend as much time on the Talmud as the Mirrer students.

Members of the Mirrer Yeshiva looked and dressed much like the other refugees, except that their heads were always covered by a hat or skullcap. But the Lubavitcher and Lubliner Chassidim looked very different from anyone else in Shanghai. Outdoors, in any kind of weather, their heads were always covered by large black hats, under which a skullcap could often be seen sticking out. The Chassidim never wore neckties, and their clothing consisted of dark pants and caftans rather than jackets. The caftans, dark frocks reaching to the knees, looked like a combination of a jacket and coat with a slit down the center in the back beginning at the waist. Their tsitsis, a garment worn by men with fringes on its four corners, usually could be seen sticking out of the slit in their caftans. The Chassidim shaved their heads, but were bearded and had long sidelocks that were sometimes tied up and tucked behind their ears. I had seen Chassidim dressed just like that on visits to my mother's family home in Poland, but was surprised to find them suddenly in the streets of Shanghai. After their arrival, it was pretty funny to see the Chassidim dressed in their traditional garb being pulled through the streets of Hongkew in rickshaws.

The story behind the new arrivals' journey to Shanghai amazed me. They escaped from Poland just ahead of the Germans and fled to the city of Kovno (now Kaunus) in Lithuania. Since the Germans captured Poland quickly and seemed ready to overrun Lithuania as well, the Jews in Kovno searched frantically for ways to escape. A yeshiva student from Holland visited the Dutch consul in Kovno. The student got the consul to write a note into his passport saying that no visa was needed to travel to Curacao, a Dutch colony in the Caribbean. Of course, since Curacao was a Dutch colony it was not surprising that Dutch citizens could travel there without needing a visa. Chiune Sugihara, the Japanese consul in Kovno, then gave the Dutch student a transit visa to cross Japan on his way to Curacao.

The Dutch student's colleagues in the yeshiva, as well as the other Jews who had escaped to Kovno, had few official papers other than their passports from the Polish consul saying that they were Polish citizens. Nevertheless, they talked the acting Dutch consul into writing the information about Curacao into their passports, which they took to Sugihara. The Japanese consul asked no questions and simply stamped them with transit visas allowing the refugees to enter Japan en route to Curacao. The new arrivals felt that Sugihara was kind to them because he must have known that no one could actually reach the Dutch colony in the Caribbean. The transit visas made it possible for the refugees to cross the Soviet Union on the Trans-Siberian Railroad to Vladivostok, Russia's port in the Far East. There, they boarded a Japanese ship to Kobe, a port city in Japan. Since they had no way of continuing their journey to Curacao, the refugees remained in Kobe until the Japanese deported them to join the rest of us in Shanghai.

During their first few days in Shanghai the newly arrived yeshiva students lived at Beth Aharon. My father and I visited Beth Aharon a few days after these refugees' arrival. The Torah scrolls and most of the seats had been removed from the synagogue's main hall and cots set up for the students. We wandered through the aisles and spoke to some of the young men in Yiddish. They looked very pale, as if they never got out into the sun, and were quiet. The students answered most questions in one or two words and seemed confused to suddenly find themselves in Shanghai.

In the next few weeks most of the yeshiva students found places to live in Hongkew. We were pleased when the *mashgiach* (spiritual supervisor) Reb Yechezkel Lewenstein, who was one of the revered leaders of the Mirrer Yeshiva, his wife, and two daughters as well as their husbands rented the remaining rooms in our house on Seward Road.

The arrival of the yeshivas suddenly brought the war in Europe home to us. Until then, it had all seemed distant to me because the war reports came from places I had never heard of. My parents, however, followed the news about the war in Europe anxiously. Since the new arrivals had left Poland a long time ago they also could not tell us very much about what was now happening to the Jews there. Without any mail from Europe, all we could do was worry.

On December 7, 1941, the war suddenly reached our doorstep. The thunder of exploding shells and rattling windows woke us that night. For what seemed like a long time, though it may have been only a few minutes, we heard loud whining sounds that began in the distance, came toward us, and ended in an explosion that echoed all over Hongkew. Then, the same whine started somewhere nearby and became quieter before ending in another explosion far away from us. We gathered in frightened knots on the ground floor of our house; my parents kept telling me to stay away from the windows and not to turn on any lights. Some people guessed that we were hearing exploding cannon shells, while others thought they might be bombs.

The next day we learned that the Japanese in Hongkew had opened fire on one American and one British navy ship that had been tied up in the harbor near the International Settlement. The two ships had returned the fire until they were sunk. Rumors spread that the ships' crews had surrendered to the Japanese. That day the German radio news broadcast in Shanghai declared a great Japanese victory at Pearl Harbor and proudly announced that Japan had entered the war on the side of the Third Reich. In Shanghai the Japanese army marched across the creek separating Hongkew from the other parts of the city and took over the International Settlement and the French concession. They now ruled all of Shanghai.

The surrender of the American and British sailors quickly became real to us. Shanghai had one of the largest jails in the world located less that a block away from Oihel Moshe. For some time after December 7 groups of heavily armed Japanese soldiers with bayonets fixed to their rifles surrounded the jail and also took up positions on the corner of Ward and Chusan Roads, the center of refugee life in Hongkew. There were some European style cafes on Chusan Road, where people whiled away the time reading the newspapers, sipping cups of tea or coffee, and talking with other refugees. On December 8 Japanese soldiers set up a machine gun post near the steps of the cafe on the corner of Chusan and Ward Roads, aimed directly at the prison.

We guessed that the sailors who had surrendered to the Japanese were being held in the jail. Behind their backs, some refugees made fun of the Japanese soldiers and wondered how a small group of unarmed British and American sailors could escape from such a mighty prison and get lost among the Chinese residents of Shanghai. The Japanese must have realized the same thing because after a few weeks the troops around the prison disappeared and life returned to what had become normal for us.

My parents and other adults continuously discussed what Japan's entry into the war meant for us and for the progress of the war. Some people felt that nothing much had changed because Hitler could not work with any other government for very long, and certainly not with an Asian government like Japan's. Problems between the new allies were sure to arise and might actually help the refugees. Others were frightened that the Germans would pressure the Japanese to persecute us, just as the Nazis had. These speculations were repeated among my friends, but since nothing seemed to change we soon found other things to think about.

For the first few months after the Japanese entered the war our life in Shanghai continued much as before. Now that they controlled all of Shanghai, the Japanese removed the hut on the Garden Bridge that used to mark the border between Hongkew and the International Settlement. American and British citizens living in the city were ordered to wear red armbands on their coats or jackets. A picture of the Stars and Stripes was on the armbands of Americans, and the Union Jack appeared on those worn by the British.

The British police officers in the International Settlement had always ridden around Shanghai in cars and rickshaws acting as if they were too important to see anyone. We were not unhappy to notice that these officers suddenly became hard to find, and when discovered seemed quite meek. Of course we remembered that these officers had not permitted refugees to enter Shanghai when the ships from Europe had tied up in "their" section of the city. Many of the Indian sergeants and policemen did not seem as ramrod straight as they used to be either. Like the British officers, the Indians now also seemed eager to shrink into the walls. The officers and ordinary policemen in the settlement avoided contact with the Japanese almost as much as we and the Chinese did. The Japanese strutted all over Shanghai and bossed everyone around. They were as cruel to the Chinese as they had always been, but now there was no way the Chinese people could avoid Japanese rule anywhere in Shanghai.

What was most important to us was that the Japanese seemed to pay little attention to the Jewish refugees. We hoped that being ignored meant that they did not quite know what to do with us. The refugees who had arrived from Kobe said that they were treated well in Japan. That gave us hope that little would change now that the Japanese had entered the war. When we first arrived in Shanghai the Chinese called us *nakuning*, or foreigners, though they seemed somewhat surprised to find us living right next to them in the poorest parts of town. It pleased many of us, who were used to being treated as outcasts in Germany, to be called foreigners just like all the other

Europeans in Shanghai. As they became more familiar with the refugees, the Chinese began referring to us as *jutaning*, or Jews, rather than
merely as foreigners.

A few months after the outbreak of the war the British and Americans disappeared from the streets of Shanghai. A wave of fear spread
among the Jewish refugees when we heard that they were held in concentration camps outside of town. While the refugees continued to
be left alone, we worried about what the Japanese now had in store
for us.

An announcement by the Japanese ordered that a civilian guard,
called Pao Chia, should be formed in each of the lanes. The adult men
in each family took turns standing guard every night. They wore white
armbands with the Chinese letters for Pao Chia and were given night
sticks while on duty. In our lane the large iron gates leading to Broadway were closed late at night and the men on guard duty sat near the
gates, when they were not checking the houses in the lane. No one ever
said exactly from whom the Pao Chia was supposed to protect us, but
the sight of our fathers standing guard, wearing official looking armbands, and carrying night sticks seemed exciting. The adults smiled
nervously about the Pao Chia and sighed deeply while wondering what
the future held for us.

Soon the first signs appeared indicating that the war would bring
many shortages. To save gasoline for the Japanese army the gas company was ordered to convert its cars and trucks to run on the same
fuel we used for our gas stoves. A converted vehicle was conspicuous
because the fuel was carried in a box on the roof. These fuel contain-
ers were about a foot high, as long and wide as the vehicles, and covered with a heavy piece of rubberized canvas. The canvas was stretched
taut after the vehicles were refueled and began to sag noticeably as the
gas was used up. The cars got more fuel by filling up at any of the gas
pipes in the city. Gas company cars often pulled up for a refill at the
gas line near the entrance of our lane. A crowd usually gathered when
the driver opened the pipe to fill up. The children were then chased

away, so that we would not breathe too much of the gas escaping during the refueling. At first it was exciting to smell the odor of gas before it evaporated, but after a while we got used to it.

Since most of the yeshiva students had rented rooms in Hongkew, the leaders of the Mirrer Yeshiva searched for a building nearby for its headquarters. In the meantime, the yeshiva students joined in Oihel Moshe's three daily prayer services and also studied there during the day. The students felt at home in Oihel Moshe because it was the only Orthodox synagogue in Hongkew, and most of the synagogue members also came from Eastern Europe and spoke Yiddish.

We ran into the yeshiva students every day on our way to the Talmud Torah, which met on the third floor of the synagogue. Many of the students were interested in what we were studying. I was standing on the steps of the entrance to the synagogue one day when Reb Chaskell, one of the older and most respected students, asked me what I had been learning. Reb Chaskell was a tall man who had the deep-set eyes of someone who did a great deal of reading, and his skin was very pale as if he never got into the sun. He usually started to study after evening prayers were completed and we heard that he stayed at it through most of the night. Whenever I saw him outside of the synagogue, Reb Chaskell was smoking, and his fingers and teeth had reddish tobacco stains all over them. Gradually, some other students gathered around us and I quickly became the center of attention as five or six yeshiva students took turns peppering me with questions or posing problems about what I had learned. After I answered the first few easy questions, they began to ask more difficult ones that called for putting things together to find the answers. After a while the questions became even more difficult. I took some chances and tried to answer the really difficult questions by thinking about what we had learned and figuring out wha. the next steps could be, even though we had covered very little of that material during our lessons. I felt excited when the students accepted my answers and followed them up with more questions, leading me even further afield from what we had been studying.

The students continued questioning me for about half an hour, though the time flashed by so quickly that it seemed to have been only a moment or two. I was enjoying the session until the questions became too difficult for me, and I had to admit that I could not answer them. At that point Reb Chaskell, who had led the questioning and was smoking continuously throughout the session, came to my defense, "That's not a fair question to ask him! Some of us would have trouble dealing with that." With that the questioning stopped, and Reb Chaskell turned away remarking, "He has a good head."

I was delighted to hear that. I did not remember much about the kindergarten I went to in Berlin or if I had any difficulty learning there. The teachers at the Kadoorie school were unhappy with me, however, and I was getting poor grades in almost all my subjects. After summer camp I began to have even more trouble with my school work. I learned to speak English quite easily and had no trouble starting to read it, but writing was hard work and frustrating for me. It was almost painful to force my hand to write the letters neatly and correctly. One day I finished writing my first complete sentence in school. I had a lot of trouble keeping the few words on a straight line and even though I began on the first row of the sheet, my hand wandered and the sentence ended on the third line. When I proudly brought the sheet home to my mother, she was shocked and asked me, "Is that the best you can do?"

My parents and the teachers at the Kadoorie school always lectured me that I was not paying enough attention in class. I tried to listen, but my mind always seemed to wander. The teachers at SJYA made us do a lot of memorizing. I did not like having to memorize spelling lists, multiplication tables, the meanings of words, the places of cities on maps, or an endless number of other things. The assignment I hated most was memorizing long and complicated rules of English grammar. When I worked on my homework, my parents left our room in order not to distract me, but it was still difficult for me to sit in one spot and concentrate for long periods on the assignment. Written tests in school were especially difficult for me and I always tried to finish them as quickly as possible, even though I sometimes knew that my answers were wrong. No one ever said it to me directly, but I knew that the teachers thought I was a slow student. My mother always told me that I was smart and could do well if I would only concentrate and try harder. I began to realize that deep down my mother was starting to worry that she might be wrong about me.

I felt almost giddy with pride and excitement when I rushed home to tell my parents how well I had done in answering the yeshiva students' questions. Even before the yeshiva had arrived in Shanghai, I had always been a much better student in the Talmud Torah than at the Kadoorie school. We spoke only Yiddish there, and that made me feel very much at home. I also liked the way we studied because no one ever worked alone. After the teacher explained something, we went over it with another student or with the whole group. A lot of our work in the Talmud Torah involved figuring things out. We would read a few sentences in one of the five books of Moses and then study commentary about what the sentences might mean; the comments, in a different type of print, were found right below the text. One commentator, Rashi, was often interesting because he said that there were many different, and sometimes surprising, ways of looking at what the Bible said. At other times Rashi showed how the passage we were reading was related to others that seemed to have little to do with it. I liked that and was always good at explaining the Bible or Rashi's comments to the other students or answering the teacher's questions. The work was completely different in the Kadoorie school, where I hardly ever answered any questions correctly in class and couldn't explain anything to anyone. After all the trouble I had learning how to write at SJYA, I was especially happy that we never did any writing in the Talmud Torah.

My parents were always pleased to hear that I was doing well in the Talmud Torah. Whenever she got a good report about me from one of the teachers, my mother lectured me that it proved I was not really applying myself at the Kadoorie school. She kept telling me again and again that learning to read Hebrew and to understand the Bible and being able to read Rashi was much more complicated than anything taught at SJYA. However, even though I knew that she was probably right, my mother's lectures did not help me learn anything at the Kadoorie school more easily. After many discussions, my parents arranged for one of my teachers from SJYA to tutor me twice a week.

After that first session with the yeshiva students, I often looked for other informal tests. My answers were not always as excellent as they had been that first time, but word soon got around the yeshiva that I was pretty smart. Many of the yeshiva students seemed happy to take time out from their studies to answer questions and explain things to me, and often looked for me in the synagogue to read a paragraph or two and point out different things about them. At those times they mentioned that since I was good at it, I should think about full-time study in the yeshiva.

When I told my parents that I wanted to go to the yeshiva and drop out of the Kadoorie school, they became angry and would not even talk about it. I knew that they were glad that I was doing so well in my Hebrew studies, but they reminded me that yeshiva students were the poorest people in Poland. My mother kept telling me about life in Szendiszov, the small Polish town in which she was born. Her family owned an egg business and always gave charity to the yeshiva students who could not make a living on their own. She mentioned time and again how her parents usually invited some yeshiva students for dinner on the sabbath and on holidays; the meal they shared with her family was often the best food and sometimes the only complete meal those students had all week. Did I want a life of waiting to be invited to eat at the homes of strangers in order not to starve? We had many arguments about that. My parents took turns pleading, urging, and insisting that I continue both at the Kadoorie school and at the Talmud Torah in the afternoon. If I would only concentrate a little more on my English studies, my mother urged me all the time, I would be a well-balanced person, a knowledgeable Jew—and successful in life.

My parents' urging and the tutoring I was getting did not help me improve my poor grades at the Kadoorie school or my feelings about being forced to go there. I began to feel less and less comfortable at the school and found myself more and more distant from the other students. It seemed as if the only time I truly came to life in school was when I went to the Talmud Torah.

5   Ghetto

On February 18, 1943, the Japanese authorities issued a proclamation ordering all the refugees to live in a "restricted area" in a small part of Hongkew. We immediately called this a ghetto. All the refugees living outside the boundaries of the area were ordered to move inside the ghetto within three months. Nothing was said about how the people living outside the ghetto would find housing inside the borders. The area of the ghetto was in the heart of Hongkew, away from the harbor. Our house on Broadway was thus well outside the ghetto limits. The house on Seward Road was located two blocks away from the harbor, also outside of the ghetto boundary. Suddenly, we had only three months to find a new place to live for us and for all of our tenants.

My parents, and all the other refugees who had to move, began to search frantically for houses inside the ghetto limits. Everyone realized that it would be easiest to exchange houses with Chinese or Japanese families living within the ghetto borders. Before the proclamation the area within the ghetto was considered to be even poorer than the other parts of Hongkew. Now, because we were forced to move, houses in the ghetto suddenly became much more valuable than those outside, and an even exchange of dwellings could not be arranged.

The homes of the Chinese people willing to trade houses with refugees were much smaller than ours and did not have enough room for all our tenants. The owners of houses that were about the same size as ours insisted on being paid "key money" before they would agree to trade houses. My parents discussed these problems with our tenants, and they agreed to share the cost of the key money. We finally found a house on Wayside Road inside the ghetto in a lane that was much smaller and dirtier than our present one on Broadway. The Wayside Road house had one more room than we needed; it was a tiny chamber separated from a larger room by a thin wooden wall that did not reach the ceiling. Since this room had very little privacy my parents hoped to rent it to some yeshiva students, who were hardly ever at home and spent all day and much of the evening in the yeshiva.

The Chinese people living in the house on Wayside Road wanted a lot of key money before they agreed to trade houses. We found two yeshiva students willing to rent the tiny room and after a lot of bargaining my parents and the Attermans decided that, with the additional rent from the new tenants, we could afford the house in the ghetto. We agreed to the exchange, even though we were especially unhappy about one feature of the new house. There were no water toilets; the Chinese occupants used a covered bucket in each of their rooms. We set aside one tiny, dingy room on the ground floor in the back of the building as a toilet for all the residents and built two separate stalls for waste buckets. The waste was collected every day before dawn. It was agreed that everyone would take turns admitting the Chinese workers who picked up the waste buckets at 4:30 in the morning. The workers emptied the buckets into wheelbarrows that they pulled through the lanes. The stench remained long after they were gone.

While not having water toilets was difficult for us and many of the refugees who moved into the ghetto, we learned that some Chinese people had the opposite problem. A few refugees reported that when they returned to their old houses for some reason they found that the new Chinese residents had installed the smelly toilet buckets next to the water toilets, while others had removed the water toilets entirely and turned the space into a little room.

No one was happy about the toilet facilities in the house on Wayside Road, but otherwise all the tenants agreed that it would be a reasonable trade. The new house also had a common kitchen and an electric stove. The new lane was in a good location, only a short walk away from Chusan Road, which was still the center of refugee life. It was also close to the new headquarters of the Mirrer Yeshiva. Each family still had a private room in the new house, but their rooms were either a little smaller or a bit larger than the ones they had on Broadway. There was a lot of bargaining about who would get which rooms and about the amount of key money people would have to pay.

One married couple had a special problem. They had twin beds that would not fit into their room in the new house—the room was even too small for a double bed. They agreed that the husband would sleep on a sofa placed in the corridor at night. Every morning they removed the bedding and kept it in their room while the sofa was stored flat against the wall of the corridor during the day. I wondered how this man would manage to sleep when the workers walked by him early every morning with the smelly toilet buckets or when people came home late at night and passed his bed to get to their rooms. Because their new room was so tiny and their life so uncomfortable this couple paid less key money than the other tenants. All these problems were solved in time for us to move inside the ghetto limits a few days before the deadline. Except for one other house also occupied by refugees, all the buildings in our new lane had Chinese residents. My parents and the Neufelds were able to arrange for a similar exchange of the house on Seward Road with another house on Wayside Road.

Near our new house, as in many of Shanghai's other poorest sections, we found a shop selling boiled water. Since tap water was not drinkable the Chinese, and now many refugees, bought boiled water for coffee, tea, cooking, and drinking. Rationing of electricity after Pearl Harbor made it cheaper to buy boiled water than to heat water on our electric stove. At mealtimes, a long line of people curled around these shops. Each store had a coal-fired stove with three large cauldrons, and one of these was usually boiling. When the water had come to a boil the owner scooped it out with a large dipper and poured the boiling water into our thermos bottles, which would keep it hot until the next day. The water was so cheap that we didn't pay for it with money; instead we bought a bunch of bamboo tokens and used one every time we had a thermos filled. Sometimes water carriers heaved two heavy buckets of water out of the store to some lucky person's house for a bath.

Since only Jewish refugees were ordered to move into the ghetto, some refugees were urged to convert to Christianity to avoid being forced to move into the ghetto. Robert Knopp, a boy I got to know slightly after he moved into the ghetto, lived in a house in the French concession along with five other Jewish refugee families. Shortly after the ghetto was created, a Chinese man went from door to door in Robert's house and urged the Jewish refugees to convert to Catholicism. Families agreeing to be converted were offered fifty American dollars, in addition to getting a certificate saying that they were Catholics and would not have to move into the ghetto. Even though fifty American dollars was a great deal of money, none of the refugees in Robert's house accepted the offer, although we heard that some other families did convert.

After the order to move into the ghetto was announced, we heard nothing more from the authorities. Some people felt that the Japanese may never have been really serious about forcing us to move. They guessed that the Japanese created the ghetto to impress their new allies but did not really care whether we moved. These people seemed to be right because the Japanese continued to pay little attention to us and ignored the few refugees who continued to live outside the ghetto limits after the deadline had passed. My parents and the many others who had exchanged nicer houses for smaller, dirtier, and more expensive ones inside the ghetto started to wonder if we had moved too hastily.

The guessing about how the Japanese felt lasted for only three months. One day the head of every Jewish refugee family still living outside the ghetto borders was jailed. Word spread rapidly that the conditions in the jail were awful, even by Shanghai standards. The Jewish prisoners were held in the same cells as Chinese criminals, they were given very little food, and the jail was infested with lice and rats. After less than two weeks, all the refugee prisoners became terribly sick and were released one by one. They were immediately taken to the hospital for the Jewish refugees that had been set up in the Ward Road Heim.

We heard that the released refugees had very high fevers and had become infected with typhoid. We guessed that the lice in the prison spread the illness, because all of the released prisoners had the same disease. In the next ten days all but one of the former prisoners died. After that no one thought that the Japanese had forgotten about us or that they did not care if we obeyed their orders. Fear that we might not be much better off with the Japanese than we had been with the Germans spread among the refugees.

Many refugees had jobs in offices or shops outside the ghetto. Anyone who needed to travel out of the ghetto, for work or for any other reason, had to apply to the Japanese authorities for permission. These people received a pass and also had to wear a round metal pin on their coats or jackets as a sign that they had a permit to move around Shanghai. The pins were about the size of a big button and came in three colors. Blue buttons meant that the wearer could leave the ghetto during business hours for one month; green buttons were given for a week's permit and yellow ones for a one-day pass.

We began to realize that the ghetto solved many problems for the Japanese. They probably could not find any camp big enough for the large number of refugees; people guessed that there were about 16,000 of us now living in the ghetto. If the Japanese had locked us up in a concentration camp along with the Americans and the British, they would have had to provide for us, whereas in the ghetto we had to look after ourselves. The Japanese did not even have to guard the boundaries. Except for the few Germans and a larger group of Russians who remained free to wander all over Shanghai, how could anyone with a European appearance travel in a city filled with Chinese and Japanese people?

The boys attending the Talmud Torah with me had a special reason to be thankful that the Russian Jews were living outside of the ghetto. In early October we were told that every boy would get a present of a new pair of shoes for Chanukah. A Chinese man came to the school and after removing our shoes, traced the outline of our feet with a pencil on a piece of paper. On the first day of Chanukah the Chinese man returned with Joseph Tukachinsky, a wealthy Russian Jew, carrying a huge bundle of new shoes. In a ceremony Tukachinsky then gave every boy a new pair of shoes as a Chanukah present. These became our "good shoes" and at first we wore them only on the sabbath or holidays.

Kanoh Ghoya, a Japanese official who spoke some English, was put in charge of the Jews in the ghetto. Ghoya was extremely short—he seemed to be no taller than I, and I was only ten years old. Ghoya was a civilian, not part of the Japanese army, but he walked stiffly with his back ramrod straight. Ghoya was always dressed correctly in a suit and tie and had a thin, neatly trimmed mustache. He was supposed to look tiny behind the huge desk in his large office at the police station. Refugees had to apply to Ghoya for passes to leave the ghetto. We heard that people waited in long lines for many hours at the police station before they could enter Ghoya's office.

Rumors spread among the refugees that Ghoya was taking violin lessons from one of the Austrian Jews in the ghetto. One day Ghoya was said to have admired a picture of Napoleon in the violin teacher's house. We heard that while gazing at the picture of the little French emperor Ghoya took an even more military pose than usual and said, "That was a great man, but I am a greater one. I am the king of the Jews."

Ghoya had an exact notion of how politely the refugees should act toward him. There was a rumor among the refugees that a woman had applied to him for a one-day pass to leave the ghetto. It was an extremely hot and humid day, and the woman wore an outfit with a bare midriff. Ghoya asked her why she was dressed that way. The woman became flustered and answered that she had difficulty coping with the heat. Ghoya is supposed to have said, "Oh, I see, you are hot," and ordered that a pail of water be brought to him. Then he doused the stunned woman with the water, saying, "In the future, you will dress more respectfully when you come to my office." He then threw her out of the police station.

We heard rumors that Ghoya screamed and mistreated refugees who came to his office and that he sometimes kicked and slapped some of them. Other stories were told of Ghoya acting nicely toward children and older refugees. My parents were glad that they never had to visit Ghoya's office. They told me to avoid him, and if I couldn't avoid him to avert my eyes so that he would not notice me. I sometimes saw Ghoya at matches between soccer teams in the refugee's league. At that time he was usually striding up and down the sidelines with an air of someone who knew a great deal about the game.

As the war continued our lives became more difficult. Many types of food, such as butter, margarine, and meat, became expensive. My parents always cut the fat off any chicken or beef and heated it until it melted. We saved the fat in jars and spread it on our bread at home and on the sandwiches that I took to school. When I ate my lunch at the Kadoorie school, some of the kids who did not have enough to eat sometimes asked me to give them a sandwich. That was always difficult for me. My parents did not want me to give precious food away, but I could not refuse to share with another kid whose family could not even afford to make him a sandwich. I generally told the kids who asked for food that I could share once in a while, but not every day because we did not have enough food either. Fortunately, the same kids usually did not ask me to share my lunch again.

I continued trying to change my parents' mind about letting me drop out of the Kadoorie school so that I could spend all my time studying at the Mirrer Yeshiva. My mother kept repeating that she had not left her home in Poland for Berlin and then escaped to Shanghai only to have me return to the life of a yeshiva student as if we lived in a Polish shtetl. However, I continued to get very poor grades in every subject at the Kadoorie school and did very well in my Hebrew studies. I was especially glad that no one in the yeshiva ever made fun of me because of my crooked head and that the senior students were actually eager to help answer any questions I had about what we were studying. In the fall of 1942, a few months before my tenth birthday, my parents finally agreed to have me leave the Kadoorie school, and I started to attend the Mirrer Yeshiva full-time.

A number of the children of other refugee families, who had arrived in Shanghai before the Mirrer students, also joined the yeshiva. Rumors spread that somehow the yeshivas were receiving money from abroad. Food had become extremely expensive once the war started. Most Orthodox Jews shopped in a couple of stores that sold kosher food and in an open air market two blocks away from Oihel Moshe. When my mother went shopping for food during the week, she could afford to buy only a few eggs, a half-quart of milk, and sometimes two ounces of butter. My parents did not eat these expensive foods but insisted that my body needed them so that I would grow up healthy. It was always difficult for me to swallow my buttered bread or to drink milk while my parents watched, without sharing any of it. Every once in a while I saw one of my parents licking a few remaining crumbs from the plate after I finished eating, before washing the dishes.

My mother told me that the wives of yeshiva families seemed to be buying all the meat, milk, and butter that they could possibly use, in addition to ordering large bottles of very expensive sweet cream.

The difference between the other refugees and the people from the yeshivas was particularly clear on Fridays, when religious families shopped for the sabbath. My mother always came home from the market and wondered how the yeshiva families could afford to buy expensive chickens and large portions of beef, while many of the other refugee families made do without any meat at all. Although I never talked to my parents about this directly I realized that their worry about having enough food for me must have helped to convince them to let me leave the Kadoorie school. They must have hoped that the yeshiva would share some of the money being sent to them once I became a full-time student there. I kept urging my best friend Sigi Loebel to convince his parents to let him join me in the yeshiva, and even though they refused at first, it was not long before Sigi also left the Kadoorie school. I guessed that Sigi's parents had the same worries about having enough food.

In the yeshiva I soon learned about a number of sins of which I had been unaware before. We were taught that it was wrong to waste time on many of the things we used to do for fun before joining the yeshiva, since that time could be spent in study of the Torah or Talmud. It was considered a waste of time to play games or take part in sports when that time could be spent reviewing what we were studying. We were also told that it was not fitting for a yeshiva student to seem interested in girls or to be seen in their company. It was not even considered fitting to think about girls, since that time could be spent in study. I tried very hard to avoid such sinful thoughts and deeds and felt guilty whenever I caught myself having a fantasy about any of the pretty girls in the ghetto or about many of the bar girls we saw around Hongkew.

One of the young women about whom I had many a sinful thought lived in our house. Irma was an attractive, wonderfully shaped young woman in her midtwenties. She and her parents had a little dog named Daisy; before entering the yeshiva I often played with the puppy. Now that I was a yeshiva student such play was clearly a waste of time that could more profitably be spent in study. It was easy for me to ignore Daisy, but not watching or thinking about Irma was much more difficult. Her parents did not have jobs or other means of earning a living, and Irma supported them by working as a bar girl. She usually left for work after dinner; some nights she came home very late and at other times I never heard her return at all. Even without seeing Irma, the smell of her perfume was enough to give me a clear image of what she looked like.

In the heat of the summer Irma often walked around the area of our shared kitchen dressed only in the skimpiest underwear from which her lovely breasts and hips continually threatened to escape. I became more aware of Irma after we moved to the ghetto because she and her family now had the room immediately to the right of ours; in our old house on Broadway they lived on the floor below us. I could easily look into Irma's windows from our room, and I was ashamed of the amount of time I spent trying to steal a glimpse of her dressing through whatever crack I could find in our curtains and in theirs. I knew that my thoughts about Irma and my trying to peek at her were most certainly not fitting for a yeshiva student. It also bothered me that Irma often appeared in my dreams on many steamy and restless nights. I prayed deeply and with great feeling to seek forgiveness for my sinful thoughts and dreams about Irma.

We knew that Irma and a number of the young women in the ghetto were working in the bars to earn a living. There were also whispered rumors that some women from Heime were working in the shops empty of everything but women, while others were supposed to be entertaining Japanese soldiers in their rooms. One Sunday afternoon my parents and I visited a family we had known in Berlin. The husband was a little older than my parents and, like them, had come from Poland; he also attended services at Oihel Moshe. Their daughter was a blonde, heavy-set woman who always seemed to have a sad and somber face. She moved slowly and usually answered questions in a word or two, when she spoke at all. We thought that this woman was feeling depressed because her husband had been unable to join her in Shanghai. Their son was a few years younger than me and was in a lower grade of the Kadoorie school. This family seemed better off than the rest of us. They lived in a large house and had the use of the whole lower floor for their family, rather than just one room.

We were drinking some tea during our visit with this family when a Japanese soldier drove up in a small military truck and walked toward the house. The daughter seemed a little embarrassed and then got up and disappeared into the rear of the house, excusing herself by saying that she had to take care of something with the Japanese man. My parents seemed confused for a moment, while the woman's son invited me outside for a walk with him. I asked the boy who the Japanese man was and he looked away from me saying, "He's my mother's friend. . . . She has many friends."

Shortly after that, my parents came striding out of the house to collect me. As we walked away from the family's house, my parents told me not to have anything to do with that boy again. It did not take me long to figure out why that family was better off than the rest of us.

6   *A Yeshiva Student in Shanghai*

*A*ll the other yeshivas also found quarters in the ghetto. The Lubliner and Lubavicher Chassidim found small houses in different lanes in the ghetto. The Mirrer Yeshiva continued to study in Beth Aharon for some time and eventually made its headquarters on Wayside Road, not far from our house in the ghetto. The yeshiva bought two attached houses and knocked down the walls to create one large building with a big auditorium on the second floor. All the prayer services were held in that hall, and we also gathered there to study. My parents continued to attend religious services at Oihel Moshe on Saturdays and holidays, but my friends and I stayed at the yeshiva for all prayer services. Other than my parents, their friends, and our neighbors, most of the people with whom I had any contact were part of the yeshiva, and now all my friends also studied there. I had almost nothing to do with any of the other refugee kids, even those who used to be in my classes at the Kadoorie school.

All the new students formed a small group called the *yeshiva ketana* (small yeshiva). In the Talmud Torah we had usually studied different parts of the books of Moses and the commentaries about the Bible. In the yeshiva we advanced to study the Talmud, which dealt with the general and religious laws Orthodox Jews were required to obey. Each of the laws was usually based on a sentence, and sometimes even on a single word, in the Bible. In the Talmud Torah, the commentaries on the Bible were often difficult. Now in the yeshiva things became much more complicated than anything I had studied before, either at SJYA or in the Hebrew school.

Rabbi Finkelstein, who was well known as a scholar and teacher of the Talmud, lectured to the students in the *yeshiva ketana* for an hour and a half every day to help us understand this difficult material. He covered a section of a page in the volume we were studying and went over the commentaries dealing with the selection. The rest of the day was spent in the main hall of the yeshiva, where we paired up with other students to review the selection we had studied in the group lesson. Rabbi Abraham Aaron Kreiser, one of the scholars in the yeshiva, offered to help me with my studying and met with me almost every day for an hour or two. During these sessions he showed me new ways of looking at the material we were studying and pointed out their relationships to other topics. He was always delighted when I grasped some complicated question rapidly and often told me that I could become a very good student of the Talmud if I continued to apply myself. Every one of the other students in the small yeshiva had one of the yeshiva scholars helping him. When our private teacher was not around, the other scholars were always glad to help when we were confused or puzzled by something.

The Mirrer Yeshiva brought prayer books, Bibles, and volumes of the Talmud to Shanghai. These began to wear out from heavy use, and more books were needed both to replace them and to give to the new students. A Chinese printer copied the prayer books and volumes of the Talmud, and it was always exciting to begin another term with brand new volumes.

Every student was assigned a wooden study stand, which was about chest high and wide enough to hold the volumes we were studying so that we could rest the books on them comfortably. In addition to studying on the stands we also rested our prayer books on them during the three daily prayer services. I quickly memorized those prayers that were repeated at the three services, but used the prayer books to make sure that I would not accidentally miss anything. Sigi Loebel became my regular study partner and usually also sat next to me during the prayer services.

We spent all day in the yeshiva, beginning with early morning services and ending with the evening prayers, and only went home in the middle of the day for a quick lunch. Our day began with morning prayers in the main auditorium, and we gathered for the group lesson with Rabbi Finkelstein for an hour and half every day, usually during the midmorning. Before and after the lesson we joined the older students to study in the yeshiva's main auditorium. Reb Chaskell, the spiritual supervisor, usually studied in the front row of the auditorium facing the rest of the students fanning out in front of him in the auditorium.

During study sessions we took turns with our partners going over a section of the Talmud, and one of us was often standing and explaining something to the other by reading from the volume or enlarging on it with the commentary we had learned. We rarely studied in silence, but spent much of our time chanting, and we always used our hands to emphasize a particular point. Sigi would check on my understanding of what we were covering and sometimes ask questions, and then I would do the same while he was doing the explaining. We spent a lot of time standing or hunched over our stands while examining the Talmud. We sat down to rest occasionally and continued studying by tilting our stands so that the page we were working on could be read comfortably while seated.

At the Kadoorie school we usually studied by ourselves, and I was also alone while working on my homework for school. I remembered waiting endlessly for the clock to move while I studied at the Kadoorie school, but in the yeshiva I was always surprised at how rapidly time passed. When the time for afternoon prayers arrived, marking the end of our second study session of the day, it usually seemed as if we had started studying only a short time before that. When all the students were studying, our combined voices created a constant comforting hum of activity, often punctuated when some loud student's explanation unexpectedly rose above the din of our efforts to understand the Talmud. The sounds of our studying began in the auditorium and could be heard throughout the yeshiva's building. Whenever the windows were open, as they usually were from spring to fall, our studying could be heard down to Wayside Road, in front of the yeshiva's headquarters. The Chinese were a little curious about the din at first, as were many of the German and Austrian refugees to whom yeshivas were unfamiliar. Some of the Western European refugees clearly disapproved of the yeshiva and the din created by our studying; but even though the Chinese became accustomed to our ways, many of the disapproving refugees never seemed to.

During the week our studies ended with the late afternoon services, which were followed by the evening prayer after the sun set. After evening services we returned home for dinner with our families. I often wandered back to the yeshiva later in the evening, sometimes to study and at other times to meet some of my friends and gossip. We were in awe of several of the older students who were known to be the most brilliant Talmudic experts in the yeshiva; some of them could be found poring over their volumes late into the night, almost every night.

There was no formal study session on the sabbath or on holidays; at those times we gathered at the yeshiva for morning prayers, which usually lasted until noon. On Saturdays we returned in the late afternoon to celebrate an afternoon meal at which we ate some bread, sang *zemiroth* (special songs for the sabbath) for an hour or two, and then chanted the required grace after bread had been eaten. Before dusk we gathered for the afternoon prayers, followed by the evening prayers shortly thereafter, which concluded with the ceremony ending the sabbath.

A *mikve* (ritual bath) had been built on Ward Road, and we generally went to the *mikve* before Rosh Hashanah. The *mikve* was made of white tiled walls and was about six feet square and four feet deep. Over half of the water in the *mikve* had to be made up of rain water, collected by running the gutters from the building into the *mikve*. One of the other students in the *yeshiva ketana* once brought a boy from his lane along to the *mikve*. I felt superior to this boy, who thought the *mikve* was nothing but a small swimming pool and was completely unaware that it purified one for the high holidays. But I did have to admit that it was fun submerging myself in the cool water because it was so hot outside, and I stayed there quite a bit longer than was necessary. We had learned that women were required to go to the *mikve* at the end of their menstrual period before having marital relations with their husbands. Of course, men and women never went to the *mikve* at the same time. Even though we had hardly any contact with women, other than those in our families, it was a little thrilling to know why women used the *mikve*, but that is something I never admitted to anyone.

The prayer services for the high holy days, the ten days beginning with Rosh Hashanah and ending on Yom Kippur, were especially solemn. The days between the two holidays were called the Days of Penitence, a time of judgment for all human beings. We were told that the period began on Rosh Hashanah when God evaluated everyone's behavior and examined both their good deeds as well as the sins they committed during the previous year. One of the holiest prayers recited in the afternoon recounted that the verdicts about who would live or die during the coming year were recorded in the great book of judgment on Rosh Hashanah and sealed on Yom Kippur. During these ten days verdicts about everyone's fate could be changed for the better by special acts of penitence and devotion or for the worse by sinful thoughts and deeds. All the prayer services during the Days of Penitence took a little longer than usual, since every part of the prayer service was recited with deep feelings of awe. It often seemed as if our fate for the next year hung in the balance with every sentence of every prayer.

In the evening before the start of Yom Kippur prayer services we asked for forgiveness from each colleague we might have wronged in thought or deed during the last year, so that any of those misdeeds might be erased from our record. We gathered in the early evening before Yom Kippur and the darkening sky ushered in a day devoted to prayer and complete fasting, without food or water, ending only after sunset on the next day. Against the advice of my parents, I began to fast when I was only eleven, even though fasting was not required until after my bar mitzvah (confirmation) at age thirteen. Everyone attending services at the Mirrer Yeshiva was keenly aware of the subtlest meaning and significance of virtually every phrase in every one of the prayer services. During that whole day it often seemed as if God was monitoring every word I uttered and every thought and deed.

We learned that Ne'ilah, the final prayer service on Yom Kippur, was the last chance to alter the judgment about one's fate for the coming year. It was a time of great awe in the yeshiva. No one had eaten or drunk anything for over twenty-four hours, but that was far from our minds as we all stood for well over an hour throughout the Ne'ilah service. The holy ark containing the Torah scrolls remained open throughout Ne'ilah; it was the only time during the year that Reb Yechezkel Lewenstein, the *mashgiach*, led the service. He was a small man with a very soft voice and could barely be heard in the huge auditorium packed with all the students, but our reverence for him was so great and the moment so awesome that every word he chanted resonated loudly in everyone's mind. I felt that this man was so holy that he could speak directly into the Lord's mighty ear to persuade him to grant a positive fate for the coming year to me, my family, all the yeshiva students, and the Jewish people everywhere. Throughout Ne'ilah a haunting melody was sung at the end of every major paragraph and even though there must have been almost four hundred people in the room, it seemed as if we sang in one voice. I was convinced that the Lord could not help but listen to our prayers.

At the end of Ne'ilah the spell was broken and our minds turned to more usual concerns. While being without food was never much of a problem for me, not drinking anything for over twenty-seven hours in the late summer heat of Shanghai was difficult. On Yom Kippur it was usually still extremely hot and humid; the yeshiva's main auditorium felt even more uncomfortable because it was packed with people. Our active participation and singing during all the services throughout that day left our bodies drained and our throats parched. A man ran a little soda business on the first floor of the yeshiva building. On the sabbath and during holidays we used the honor system; we helped ourselves to soda and paid him at the end of the holiday. Before the beginning of Yom Kippur he laid in a huge supply of soda bottles, and at the end of Ne'ilah all the people from the large auditorium raced down to the ice chest to quench their thirst with large quart bottles of soda. I usually did not drink any of the soda because we really could not afford it, but after Yom Kippur I drained a quart in what seemed to be one long gulp, without removing the bottle from my lips.

A few days after Yom Kippur we celebrated the holiday of Succoth (Feast of Tabernacles) for eight days. The first two days and the last two were major holidays when work was forbidden, while people went about their usual business during the other four except for reciting special prayer services. Succoth commemorates the temporary huts in which the people of Israel lived during their years in the desert after the exodus from Egypt. Observant Jews build a *succah*, a hut with greenery for a roof and walls made of sheets suspended from bamboo poles. All regular meals are eaten in the *succah* during the holiday. In rainy weather we used to start the meal in the *succah* with the blessing over bread; once the bread was eaten it was considered a formal meal and we could finish eating indoors. We returned to the *succah* for the final grace.

A large *succah* was built at the yeshiva and the blessings over wine at the end of prayer services were said there during the week of Succoth. The few members of the yeshiva who were accompanied by their own families also built a *succah* in their homes. At my teachers' suggestion I tried to get my parents to build a *succah* on the upstairs porch, which was used mainly to dry our laundry. My parents refused during my first year in the yeshiva, feeling that we could say the blessings in the *succah* at Oihel Moshe or in the one at the yeshiva. I kept insisting that since I came home for my meals, instead of eating in the yeshiva, we needed a *succah* to fulfill the requirement of eating there during the holiday. I pointed out that it took very little to build a *succah*; bamboo was inexpensive and the leaves for the roof could be picked up from any yard. Once my parents agreed to build our own *succah*, I ate all my meals there, though they joined me only when the weather was nice.

Simchat Torah, the last day of Succoth, celebrates the reading of the last chapter in the books of Moses. One chapter of the Bible is read every Saturday during synagogue services, and the very last segment is reached every Simchat Torah. When the end of the Bible is reached, a small section from the very first chapter in the Book of Genesis is read immediately afterward to indicate that the study of Torah never ends. On Simchat Torah every adult in the synagogue is given the honor of being called to the Torah to recite the customary blessings. Adults also receive the honor of carrying one of the Torahs around the auditorium. There was joyous singing and dancing in the yeshiva as the Torahs were carried around the auditorium, with all the students snaking around the main hall behind those carrying the Torahs.

Some of the students who had studied in the yeshiva while they were still in Poland told me that Simchat Torah was an even more joyous holiday there. In Mir the students danced with the Torahs in

the streets surrounding the yeshiva building. I wondered what the reaction of the rickshaw runners, Chinese peddlers, occasional Japanese
soldiers, and neighbors of the Mirrer Yeshiva would be if we started
dancing through the streets of Hongkew. The yeshiva students must
have wondered about the same thing, because our celebration never
ventured out into the streets.

Simchat Torah is one of the few times in the year when people take
liberties with the melodies for some of the prayers. In mock awe, some
students chanted some of the prayers with the same melodies used
during Yom Kippur. Simchat Torah is also one of the few times of
the year when Orthodox Jews drink quite a lot of schnapps. When
the congregation dances around with the Torahs, people stop for shots
of schnapps here and there around the auditorium, and most everyone drinks a little more than they should. Even though we were told
that we were too young to drink schnapps, all of the younger students
sneaked a little schnapps from time to time to enter into the spirit of
the holiday, and that led to some very spirited dancing, singing, and a
feeling of oneness with the other students.

After the Simchat Torah prayer service in the yeshiva ended, I walked
over to pick up my father before heading home for lunch. He had also
celebrated the holiday with more than a little schnapps. The two of
us linked arms and hummed some of the melodies from the service
as we wended our way home. We did not walk very quickly or very
steadily that day but arrived home in a very good mood. When we
finally made our way up the stairs to our family's room, still singing,
my mother sniffed suspiciously at our breath, smiled broadly, and
immediately packed us both off to bed for a much needed nap for the
rest of the day.

The Passover holidays were exciting in different ways. Matzos were
prepared in the bakery building behind Oihel Moshe. During our first
two years in Shanghai my father helped bake the matzos using many
machines. The yeshiva students took over the building on the last two
days before the holiday to bake special matzos for the religious com-

munity. Instead of using machines we mixed the water and flour by hand, stirred the dough, and used only one machine to mix the dough more thoroughly than we could by hand. When the dough was taken out of the mixing machine, it was flattened into thin strips with rolling pins and we finally shaped the dough into individual matzos. We punched holes into them with a wheel-shaped tool with spokes before carrying them to the bakery's ovens on long poles. My teachers explained that the use of machines might cause some fermentation of the dough, which was not permitted on Passover. The hand-baked matzos were considered purer and were eaten by observant people at the seder services on the first two evenings of Passover and by some people throughout the holiday. There was a lot of singing and joking during each step in the preparation of the matzo, so even though it was hard work we all had a lot of fun doing it.

On the day before the beginning of Passover all the pots and pans that would be needed during the holiday were taken to be purified and made kosher for the holiday. My mother explained that in Poland and in Berlin we had special pots and pans that could be used only on Passover. In Shanghai we did not have the space to store another set, or the money to buy them, so our usual pots, pans, knives, spoons, and forks would have to do. A huge metal cauldron had been placed on a bunch of bricks in back of Oihel Moshe and a big fire was lit below the cauldron. Boiling water was needed for the purification, and people took turns placing their pots and pans, tied together with sturdy ropes so that they would not separate and get lost, into the cauldron for a few minutes until they were purified. The man in charge wore heavy gloves to protect his hands from the heat, and he took one of the glowing bricks out of the fire every once in a while with heavy metal tongs and placed it in the cauldron to make sure that the water was actually boiling. A great rush of smoke and sizzling water flew up when the brick was put into the cauldron.

We did have a special set of dishes and glasses that could be used only on Passover. During the rest of the year these were kept in one of the suitcases we had brought along to Shanghai. Using the new dishes and specially purified pots and pans made Passover an especially festive holiday.

On the first two evenings of Passover, during the seder services comes the retelling of the liberation of the Israelites from Egypt. My parents had always conducted seders at home and we continued to do so after I joined the yeshiva. Some of my friends went to the huge seder at the yeshiva, which was conducted for all the students without a family. They told me that it was a joyous event with a great deal of singing throughout the celebration. In the middle of the seder horseradish is eaten so that the Jews could empathize with the suffering of our people when they were slaves in Egypt. I heard that in the yeshiva large bowls heaped with horseradish were passed around, and that it was customary for students to reach into the bowl and make a fist and then eat all the horseradish they had clenched in their fist. Swallowing that much horseradish at one time made it hard to catch one's breath for some minutes, and students slapped each other on the back and plied their colleagues with wine until they recovered from the experience. Even though I always enjoyed the seders at home, I envied those who were able to attend the seders at the yeshiva.

It is also required that we drink four glasses of wine spaced evenly during the seder service. While my parents insisted that I have grape juice when I was younger, once I entered the yeshiva I drank the same sweet red wine that they did, so the seder was always a pretty spirited service. In our first few years in Shanghai my parents bought kosher wine from someone in the synagogue. Now that was too expensive, so we made our own wine. A few months before Passover my parents bought some red grapes at the market. We then extracted the juice by wrapping the grapes in a white linen napkin and squeezing it ever more tightly until all of the dark red juice had dribbled out into a big glass jar. We could never use the napkin for anything else, because the redness from the grapes remained in the napkin no matter how often it was washed. The peels of the grapes also went into the jar to help the juice ferment. The jar was covered by a clean white piece of paper, into which we had cut some slits so that air could get into the jar. For the next few months I watched the jar as a powdery layer formed over the peels; my parents told me that showed that they were fermenting. The juice eventually changed colors, alternating between cloudy and dark red. The wine we drank on Passover tasted very sweet and very good.

I spent all of the holidays at services in the Mirrer Yeshiva, but walked over to the Lubliner Chassidim to participate in their obser- vance of Shavuoth (the Feast of Weeks). That holiday celebrates the gift of the Torah to the Jewish people. It was a tradition among the Lubliner Chassidim to drink new wine on that holiday and sing songs for hours on end, some taken from prayer services and others telling of their faith and devotion. Moishe Fastak, one of the Lubliner Chas- sidim, had a wonderful voice and was known to be the best singer among Shanghai's religious Jews. Even though we did not study with the Lubliner Chassidim or were members of their community, they welcomed me and the other younger students from the Mirrer Yeshi- va to join their Shavuoth celebration. We spent the afternoon sipping sweet fresh wine, singing the songs we knew, and listening to the many others led by the beautiful voice of Moishe Fastak. As night fell the Chinese man who turned on the electric lights for the Lubliners was asked to wait so that the afternoon of song and reverence could stretch into the night.

My parents had always been Orthodox at home, eating only kosher food and performing no work in observance of the sabbath. After joining the yeshiva I was constantly reminded by my teachers that it was important to observe all the laws very precisely and, in turn, kept after my parents to do the same. Prodding my parents to practice ev- ery requirement down to the last detail caused arguments at home. For example, Jewish custom requires that men always cover their head with a hat, a skullcap, or a *kippah*. Men are not permitted to walk a distance of more than four steps without some kind of head covering. I always carried a *kippah* with me, and frequently had it tucked under my cap in case I would take my hat off and walk a few steps. Even though I urged my father to do the same, he would never agree to that, no matter how much I argued about its necessity.

I had a major argument with my parents about turning on the lights on the sabbath. During the sabbath, and on most other holidays, Orthodox Jews believe that it is forbidden to turn on any electric appliance or to turn it off. My parents paid little attention to that in Berlin or in Shanghai. They argued that creating light was forbidden in earlier times because it was hard work, and the sabbath was supposed to be a day of rest. Once electricity became available, turning on the lights did not involve any work at all, so they could not see why it should be forbidden. If there had been electricity in biblical times, they argued, turning lights on would never have been forbidden in the first place.

I answered heatedly that, as I had learned in the yeshiva, an observant Jew had to obey all the laws and was not free to choose which ones were most convenient. I also lectured them with an example that had often been used on me in the yeshiva. All the bricks in a wall are essential, and if you start removing the bricks of Judaism one by one, the wall is doomed to collapse. To please me, my parents agreed not turn any lights on or off during the sabbath while I was around; we arranged for a Chinese boy to turn our light on and off on Friday night. I suspected that my parents turned the lights off and on while I was at the yeshiva, but since I never saw them do it there was no point in arguing about it.

We often watched the Chinese observe holidays, especially their celebration of the Chinese New Year. During that holiday there were lots of bands, parades, and processions through the streets of Hongkew, but I mainly enjoyed watching groups of people pretending to be dragons. A vivid multicolored costume stretched from the first person in the procession to the last as these processions veered from one side of each major street in Hongkew to the other. The Chinese also set off lots of firecrackers during these celebrations, especially for the New Year's festival. These colorful and noisy celebrations seemed strange to me compared with the awe we felt during Rosh Hashanah and Yom Kippur. I sometimes wondered if the Chinese people watching our observance of holidays thought that they were just as strange as theirs were to our eyes.

Most evenings after returning home from the yeshiva I found myself with little to do before going to bed. As long as it was warm outside, my parents would usually sit in the lane or out on the street talking with our neighbors, and some of the other yeshiva students and I would take a walk through the ghetto. When the seasons changed and it became too cool to remain outdoors, our family usually settled down and read in our beds before going to sleep. A library had been formed in the ghetto from books many of the refugees had donated or sold. The library was especially convenient since few people had enough space in their rooms for books. Most of the library's books were in German, though there was also quite a large selection of English books. When one of us in the family finished a German book we passed it around to the others; once we had all read the book we had interesting discussions about it.

Even though I did not do well in many subjects at the Kadoorie school I had always enjoyed reading and had little difficulty with it. While I had never been taught to read German in school, it was not difficult to figure it out since the alphabet was the same as in English, so I easily read the German books from the library unless they were printed in the traditional Gothic type. We especially enjoyed reading and discussing Vicki Baum's and Lion Feuchtwanger's works. Eventually I figured out the Gothic type and read most books by Karl May, a favorite author of many German refugee teenagers.

My parents did not read English, but once I finished the German novels that interested me I started reading some of the English books from the library. I made my way through all of the Tarzan tales by Edgar Rice Burroughs and many of the English crime and mystery novels. When I finished most of those books I borrowed books on

English and American history and was struck by how differently each described the American Revolution. The British books described it much the way one would write about ungrateful children who turned on their parents. The American books, on the other hand, pictured the revolutionaries as heroes rising up to throw off the yoke of a harsh and unjust king. The differences in these descriptions made me think of the different interpretations in the Talmud that I studied in the yeshiva.

One day my mother was talking to one of my teachers in the yeshiva and mentioned to him how much I was reading during the evenings at home. The next day in the yeshiva I received a lecture on wasting my time reading books that had nothing to do with Judaism, when I could be studying the Talmud. I tried taking a volume of the Talmud home with me, but found that I could not read that while relaxing in bed, especially without my study partner. After that, I read the refugee newspaper when my parents were at home and peeked into their books only when they were not around. Occasionally they encouraged me to read something they had enjoyed and, after making them promise not to tell my teachers about it, I was happy to read the books.

In addition to the reading, I was often unhappy about the many other things I could not do after joining the yeshiva. Much of what used to be fun earlier was either strictly forbidden or considered "not fitting" for yeshiva students. We were taught that it was not fitting for us to play soccer or any other type of ball, to have friends who were not religious, or to do much of anything that did not deal with prayer or study of the Talmud. It most certainly was not fitting to have anything to do with young girls of my own age. I still watched the girls very closely out of the corner of my eye, so that no one could see that I was looking, but resigned myself to the fact that it would certainly be considered not fitting to go up and speak to them.

Wedding photo of my parents, Frieda and Moses Tobias. (Author's collection)

My mother and I in
Szendiszov in 1937.
(Author's collection)

My mother's passport
photo, 1938. (Author's
collection)

My mother and I aboard the
Conte Biancamano on the way
to Shanghai. (Author's
collection)

Exterior of one of the Heime. (Courtesy of the Leo Baeck Institute, New York)

Inside a Heim. (Courtesy of the Leo Baeck Institute, New York)

Hongkew after a typhoon. (Courtesy of the Leo Baeck Institute, New York)

Jewish refugees in the used clothes market on Kungping Road. (Courtesy of the Beth Hatefutsoth Photo Archive, Tel Aviv)

Kanoh Ghoya giving passes out of the ghetto to refugees. (Courtesy of the Beth Hatefutsoth Photo Archive, Tel Aviv)

Refugees looking through lists of Holocaust survivors for names of their relatives, 1946. (From the Archives of the YIVO Institute for Jewish Research)

Uncle Aaron and Taube in Szendiszov. I am pretending to ride Taube's
motorcycle. (Author's collection)

My parents and I in a park in Shanghai, spring 1948. (Author's collection)

My parents and I in Brighton Beach, Brooklyn, summer 1951. (Author's collection)

Picture of me (first row, first student on right) in SJYA gym class led by Leo Meyer.
(Courtesy of the Beth Hatefutsoth Photo Archive, Tel Aviv)

7 Life in the Ghetto

$\mathcal{E}$ven though the thermometer rarely dropped below freezing in Shanghai, it felt frigid during the winter of 1943. Everyone said it was a much colder winter than usual, but some people blamed our discomfort on the humidity while others insisted that the weight we had lost due to our meager diets had changed our views of the cold. The winds from the north whipped through our clothing and seeped through our ill-fitting windows and the walls of our house, which had no central heating. As one of our neighbors had warned, with little insulation in the walls or ceiling we had no protection from the icy winds. We tried to keep warm by wearing our heaviest clothing during the day; at night we ducked into the down-filled bedcovers that my parents had brought from Europe.

As the winter deepened my parents bought a small iron stove to heat our room on the coldest days. The stove was placed near the window so that the stovepipes would take up as little space as possible. One of the windowpanes was replaced by a piece of tin with a hole in the center to let the pipe run out into the courtyard. Smoke sometimes seeped out of the stovepipes, so we continually turned the pipes, bent them a little here or there, or added pieces of tin to close any gaps. We used hard coal whenever possible because it began to burn quickly and spread a pleasant warmth throughout the room shortly after the fire was lit, but most of the time our stove was fueled by charcoal, which was much cheaper and easier to get in Shanghai.

Shops all over Hongkew sold charcoal briquettes, which were made by mixing coal dust with water and pressing the mixture into egg-like shapes in an iron form much the way cookies were shaped. The stores selling charcoal often had boards of newly formed briquettes drying in the sun out front. It was much more difficult to start a fire of charcoal briquettes than one of hard coal, especially since the briquettes were often damp because they had not dried completely in the humid weather. We usually took turns fanning the stove until the coals were finally glowing, but this spread whiffs of smoke throughout the room that lingered long after the fire had died down. Our feather bedcovers seemed to soak up the musty, unpleasant smell of the charcoal fires and reeked of them through most of the winter. Even though my mother tried to air out the covers by hanging them from the windows on clear days, the smell of the charcoal fires did not seem to leave the bedcovers until spring.

On the coldest days we tacked some unused blankets or sheets up on the windows to keep the cold winds out and the heat in. Similar sheets and blankets began to appear on the windows of many of the other refugees, but we noticed that the Chinese people seemed to be more comfortable and need fewer stoves than we did. They usually wore tufted coats, jackets, and even pants during the winter, and thin wisps of cotton stuck out of their garments wherever they had been stitched. The tufted clothing seemed to keep the Chinese warm enough, but they looked bulky and uncomfortable to our European eyes, so few of us wore them.

A further winter difficulty resulted from our plumbing. Because the pipe bringing cold water to the second floor ran along the outside wall of the building it sometimes froze during the cold nights. We tried to let a little water drip from the second floor faucet throughout the night to prevent freezing, but some of the pipes froze anyway and once the pipes in a neighbor's house burst. Many of our Chinese neighbors wrapped thick bunches of straw around the pipes with string or wire to prevent some of the daytime warmth from escaping. My parents paid a Chinese worker to encase our pipe in the same way, which perhaps prevented our pipe from being damaged.

We did have an electric stove but were forbidden to use it very often because electricity was strictly rationed and extremely expensive. The electric meter for the second floor of our house was near the communal kitchen, around the corner from our room, and my parents checked it whenever they passed by. Every once in a while the dial speeded up dramatically, showing that someone must be using an iron or other electric appliance. Often we assumed that Irma was ironing the clothes she wore to work in the bar. At those times my father knocked on all the doors, and most loudly at the door of the room Irma shared with her parents, to get them to stop using the expensive electricity.

We did as much cooking as possible on top of the stoves that heated our rooms, but that was inconvenient because those stoves had room for only one pot at a time. On warmer days we, like our Chinese neighbors, cooked on portable charcoal stoves. We lit these stoves in the lane in front of our house and sometimes brought them upstairs for cooking. On humid days the smoke from the stoves hung over the lanes and adjoining streets, irritated our eyes, and made it difficult to breathe. At those times it often felt as if we were inhaling cigarette smoke, without even having to light up.

Cigarettes had become expensive along with everything else. Beggars searched for cigarette butts all over the ghetto. When they found a butt they pierced it with a nail attached to the end of a bamboo stick and dropped it into a tin can. We noticed the scavenging more now because my father, and many other refugees, could afford to buy only

Chinese cigarettes—despite my mother's attempts to make him quit smoking—which were probably made from that recycled tobacco. Some of the older yeshiva students smoked continuously while they were studying, and their fingers and teeth were always tobacco stained. I sometimes sneaked a cigarette from my father's pack and smoked it secretly when my parents were out of the house.

Food was becoming scarce and the prices of everything had gone up so much that we tried to eat dishes that were filling but not expensive. My mother cooked large pots of rice, buckwheat, or a yellowish grain that looked like tiny kernels of corn; the refugees called it *Hirse* in German but no one could figure out its English name. Before the war we had seen *Hirse* used as bird food. Sometimes we threw scraps of beef or chicken fat into the pots of grain to give the food a little flavor; at other times we sprinkled some sugar and cinnamon over the bowls of grain, but that stopped when sugar became terribly expensive.

As the war continued flour also became scarce and was often rotten. We sometimes found worms in the flour, and when my mother bought a sieve to sift it she discovered clumps of unrecognizable junk; we never dared to guess what these clumps were. Baking with the flour did not remove all of the crawling bugs because we occasionally found ugly worms in the loaves of bread bought from the bakery.

The tastiest things we ate that winter were baked sweet potatoes. Peddlers sold the potatoes on some of the main streets in the ghetto right from their ovens. The ovens were made of abandoned steel drums lined with hardened mud and a hole for ventilation had been cut into the bottom of the drum to bring air to the charcoal fire. Layers of hot potatoes rested on a grate on the upper half of the drum above the charcoal fire. When they were steaming hot and the insides had turned liquid and looked like a thick yellowish syrup they were delicious. The refugees learned from the Chinese to check the potatoes carefully in order not to burn their mouths. The potatoes were not expensive, and after eating one its warmth seemed to spread all over my body. We soon began to bake sweet potatoes in our own charcoal stoves.

I did not notice much difference in the way I looked, but my parents and many of the refugees seemed to be getting thinner all the time because their clothing had become several sizes too large for them. As the war continued and conditions became more difficult people seemed to shrink into their clothes. Food was getting scarcer and more expensive and hunger was a frequent companion for most of us. Since real milk and butter had become such luxuries we tried to substitute cheaper foods, such as milk made from soybeans—which tasted awful—or margarine—which smelled oily and was almost as expensive as butter.

My parents had often told me that in Poland yeshiva students were so poor that they were forced to rely on the charity of others to survive. The opposite was now the case in the ghetto. While most of the refugees went hungry the families of the yeshiva students bought milk, butter, bottles of cream, and most of the available kosher meat. They appeared much healthier than the rest of us. It was now taken for granted that the yeshivas were receiving money from America. Those of us who dropped out of the Kadoorie school and switched to the yeshiva full-time received some money every two weeks, which certainly helped.

In the next year or two quite a number of boys left the Kadoorie school to study in the Mirrer Yeshiva. My friend Sigi Loebel had joined the Mirrer Yeshiva shortly after me, and after some months Norbert Seiden also joined us. Both Sigi's and Norbert's families were similar to mine and at least one of their parents had originally come from Poland or Eastern Europe. They were also Orthodox Jews who attended Oihel Moshe and were about as observant as my family. On the other hand, a number of the other refugee children who joined the yeshiva had not been observant at all before life became so difficult, nor were most of their parents and families observant even now. My friends and I felt that these boys entered the yeshiva only to eat a little better than the rest of the refugees in Hongkew. Of course, we knew that it was not fitting to have such unkind thoughts about our fellow students, but we guessed that these boys would leave the yeshiva as soon as food became more easily available.

Money was scarce, so many families sold extra possessions they had brought from Europe and eventually were forced to sell items that had been really important to them. One day we saw a Chinese man pulling his rickshaw while wearing a derby hat. My friends and I thought that was very funny, but the older refugees sighed deeply and looked sad when he ran by.

Because we couldn't afford new clothing our garments soon became threadbare. I had grown quite a bit since coming to Shanghai, as had the other children in the ghetto, and could not fit into most of the clothes we had brought from Berlin. We children soon became accustomed to wearing our parents' clothes that had been shortened and altered for us. Many of the skilled Chinese and refugee tailors in the ghetto managed to make some of this used clothing look almost as good as new. Mr. Atterman, our downstairs neighbor, fixed one of these suits for me for the Passover holiday. He opened all the seams in a suit my father could no longer use, discarded the frayed parts, and then turned what used to be the inside of the garment to the outside before sewing it up again to fit me. He gave us the leftover scraps of clothing, telling my parents to save them for repairs in case I tore something. I tried on the unfinished garment a couple of times while Mr. Atterman was working on it, and after all the alterations were finished the suit looked as if it was brand new. Only another tailor could have guessed just how it had been made. Such major alterations were rarely undertaken because they were expensive and wasted the old garment. People in the ghetto grumbled that only yeshiva members could afford clothes made out of new fabrics, which they showed off to one another on holidays.

As the war went on life in the ghetto became even more difficult. A food kitchen, serving lunch and dinner, was opened for refugees who could not afford to feed themselves. Many refugees caught illnesses like typhoid and cholera, which were uncommon in Europe and from which there was little hope of recovery. Others suffered with tuberculosis, and most everyone had digestive problems of one kind or another. My parents kept saying that if we had more food it would be easier to fight off these diseases, but since no one could do much about the food many of the refugees—other than those in the yeshivas—became increasingly frail. We all worried about becoming ill.

Mr. Neufeld, my parents' partner in the second house, was hospitalized and died a few days later. He was buried in the cemetery on Baikal Road that was used mainly for Orthodox Jews. On the day of Mr. Neufeld's funeral only his wife and a handful of other adults were able to get a pass to leave the ghetto for the cemetery, which was located outside of the boundaries. Since teenagers did not need a pass to leave the ghetto, I attended Mr. Neufeld's burial and the graveside ceremonies for others whom we knew. I had many troubling dreams after attending a funeral and usually forgot them once I woke up, but I did remember frightening images of some headstones on the graves in the Baikal Road cemetery. The dreams started during my last term in the Kadoorie school.

One day in third grade I borrowed a crayon from a boy named Lothar and forgot to return it. He was out of school for the next two days and we heard that he was sick and had entered the refugee hospital in the Ward Road Heim with an extremely high fever. On the third day we were stunned to learn that Lothar had died of meningitis. Our parents were instructed to watch us carefully for any signs of fever or weakness and were told to bring us to the doctor for examination immediately in case of any problems.

I did not know what to do with Lothar's crayon. I was too embarrassed to return it to his parents and too ashamed to keep the crayon or tell anyone about it, even my parents. For some time I hid the crayon in a box where we kept some prayer books used only on the high holidays, even though I knew it was not fitting to have a crayon mixed in with these holy objects. One day when no one was watching me I took the crayon and a soup spoon and went for a walk not far from our house. I found some loose soil, scraped away a bit of it away, and then quickly tossed the crayon into it before covering it up.

Even though some of the people living in our house were born in Germany and Austria, we did not have very much to do with them outside of the usual daily greetings. All of our friends were originally from Poland and other Eastern European countries. When we were among friends my parents often made fun of the Jews from Germany and of their habits. German Jews were always called *yeckes* behind their backs. We never went to services, family celebrations, or funerals for *yeckes*. On Yom Kippur I often prayed for forgiveness for all the bad things I had said about *yeckes* throughout the year, but since everyone in the yeshiva also made fun of *yeckes*, just the way my parents did, I joined them in poking fun at the German Jews as soon as the Day of Atonement was over.

Since no one heard anything about their families in Europe we wondered endlessly whether their lives were better or worse than ours. One day after a holiday service I went to Oihel Moshe to pick up my father for the walk home. Services had just ended and I saw my father talking to Mr. Solny in the synagogue courtyard. Mr. Solny was one of the men in my father's group trying to get into Belgium; he ended up in Dachau with my father, and had arrived in Shanghai shortly after we did.

My father had his back turned to me and had not noticed me approaching. I overheard him telling Mr. Solny, "If our families are being treated like we were in Dachau, I can't believe that any of them will be able to stand that for very long." As soon as my father saw me, he changed the conversation and wished Mr. Solny a happy holiday before we left.

As we walked home that day, I thought about what my father had looked like and what he had told us after his release from Dachau. He rarely talked about Dachau, but the few things he did mention were frightening. Despite the cold that December when he was in Dachau, the prisoners slept on wooden bunks in unheated barracks that were arranged around a central area. Every day before dawn the prisoners were forced to line up in the yard, dressed only in uniforms that were little more than thin pajamas. The prisoners were beaten by the German guards for the slightest delay in lining up; often they were beaten for no reason at all. The guards ordered prisoners suffering from heart disease to step forward and then doused them with ice cold water. Many of those with heart conditions collapsed and some died immediately. After they were counted the prisoners were ordered to run around the yard in a huge circle. Since the prisoners' diet consisted of little more than watery soup and some pieces of stale bread, the forced exercise in the bitter cold quickly tired most of them, and some people slid to the ground from exhaustion. Anyone who fell was forced to remain on the ground, and the others who continued running were ordered to step on them. Anyone who tried to avoid stepping on their fallen comrades was forced to lie down next to them, to be stepped on by the circling prisoners.

I remembered that even though my father had been in Dachau for less than three weeks he looked like a shell of himself when he returned. During the day and a half that he was home in Berlin after his release from Dachau, my father stayed close to the stove and sometimes rested his hands on the heated tiles. I guessed that he hoped that the warmth of the tiles would chase the icy memories of the concentration camp away.

It usually took us only about ten minutes to walk from Oihel Moshe to our house on Wayside Road. On that day, it was a very long and a very silent ten minutes for both of us.

8 *Air Raids*

We followed the war news in the pages of the *Shanghai Jewish Chronicle* and by listening to the German-language radio broadcasts. We knew that both were censored and probably slanted in favor of Germany and Japan. People tried to read between the lines of the news reports to figure out what was really happening in the war. By 1943 and 1944 we understood that when the German-language radio broadcasts reported "reductions in the defensive perimeter to fight the enemy more effectively," they were describing a defeat and a retreat. Our guesses were confirmed when new "perimeter reductions" turned out to have been new pullbacks. We kept track of progress on the European and Asian fronts on maps some of the refugees brought along and those we had used in the Kadoorie school.

Even though we lived in China under Japanese occupation the refugees were most concerned about the war in Europe. As the war wore on we knew that Hitler's armies were finally being pushed back from the countries they had overrun at the beginning of the war. People were delighted to realize that battles were now being fought inside Germany rather than only in the occupied countries. Even though it was not a big surprise to us, we were overjoyed when Germany surrendered early in May 1945. In order not to anger the Japanese, the refugees in Hongkew celebrated Germany's defeat quietly and in private. In any event, no one felt all that happy because we were worried about the relatives and friends we had left behind in Europe, and there was no news from them or about them.

After the defeat of Germany, the refugees hoped that the Allies would try to put a quick end to the war by concentrating on the fighting in the Pacific. We knew that the Americans had pushed the Japanese out of most of the Pacific islands they had captured early in the war. We could also see that the Japanese army was suffering serious shortages. Because of the scarcity of gasoline throughout the war some civilian cars had been altered to run on cooking gas or even on charcoal. A charcoal burner was attached to the back of the car and before starting the automobile, the driver turned a crank on the burner that pumped air to the fire so that there would be enough energy to start the car. These automobiles did not run very smoothly and could be seen stalling and lurching forward in spurts. Refugees who knew about automobile engines said that these vehicles would break down rapidly and that the engines would never work well again. We realized that the Japanese were in really bad shape when they started to outfit some of their army vehicles with these charcoal burners.

At about that time the Japanese issued another proclamation ordering anyone living in a house that faced the street to dig foxholes. Fear spread through the ghetto when we realized that the foxholes must be part of a plan to prepare for a battle to defend Shanghai by house-to-house fighting. Our hopes that the war was about to end were dashed; instead we were suddenly afraid that we might soon be caught in the middle of a major battleground.

Everyone realized that an invasion of Shanghai would be much more dangerous for us than anything that had happened until now. Once the digging of foxholes began, we were not surprised to see water seeping into them as soon as they reached two or three feet below street level. The water in the foxholes reminded us that there were only two basements in all of Shanghai and none in Hongkew, or so we were told. If there was going to be an invasion it would be impossible for anyone to find shelter from the fighting since our flimsy houses would not offer much protection. The ruins of buildings shattered in the battle of Shanghai in 1937 could still be seen everywhere and made us realize that it would be difficult to survive any combat in the city. For the first time since the outbreak of the war, news of Allied advances in Asia frightened and worried us.

By 1945 the refugees in the ghetto felt worn out by the war. Many people suffered from illnesses but the doctors and the refugee hospital had little medication to treat patients. We all had frequent bouts of diarrhea after arriving in Shanghai and it got much worse as the war continued. Most of the refugees had picked up intestinal worms, probably from the poor food we were eating. Sometimes the worms could actually be seen in the stool. Since few people in the ghetto had toilets with running water, the diarrhea was especially sickening because we could see the worms wriggling in the smelly toilet buckets.

I had been having stomach problems for some time. We saw a doctor after I suffered with painful stomach cramps for a week and had to run to the toilet six and seven times a day. The doctor thought that I was probably suffering from dysentery but he had no medication to treat the disease. He gave me some liver extract injections twice a week to keep up my strength and I was told not to eat any fats or raw fruits, which were too expensive for us to buy anyway. The doctor hoped that the diarrhea would stop without treatment. I usually tried to go to the toilet in places where there were water closets, but the illness made it impossible for me to spend much time searching for water closets.

Our stomach problems made it difficult to absorb nutrients. Food had become so expensive that few people, outside of the yeshiva community, had enough to eat. Many refugees were taking their meals at kitchens in the Heime or carrying food from there to their rooms. It was common to see people hurrying home from the Heim kitchens carrying a set of small nested pots; the top one was covered by a lid and the pots were all held together by a long handle. One pot might contain soup, another some vegetables with a little meat, and the third could have some stewed fruits. I wondered if people hurried while carrying their meals so that the food would not get cold or because they were ashamed of being forced to get their meals from the emergency kitchens.

One night, after they thought I was asleep, I heard my parents whispering about how little money we had left. It was illegal to have American money, but despite that the value of any big item was usually figured in U.S. dollars, rather than in the money printed by the Japanese. Many refugees saved whatever they could in dollars, thinking that it was the only money that would have any value at the end of the war. During the last three years my parents used up their savings by trading in one dollar at a time to buy whatever we needed.

I heard my parents whispering that we had only seventeen American dollars left. While I did not know how much could be bought for seventeen dollars, their worried tones frightened me and I suddenly realized that our situation was serious. After the money was used up, my father worried that we might also have to go to the emergency kitchen. My mother whispered that I would probably get enough to eat in the yeshiva, since the students did not seem to suffer the shortages the rest of us did, but worried if she and my father would be allowed to eat at the emergency kitchen. There was always a lot of speculation among the refugees about how much money different families had hidden. With so many people being too poor to buy their own food, my parents were thought to be pretty wealthy because they were partners in two houses and collected rents from tenants. That night it took a long time, long after my parents had stopped whispering to one another, before I was able to fall asleep.

In early May 1945, when my parents worried about my diarrhea, I also developed a bad toothache. After examining me, the dentist in the ghetto said that one of my teeth would have to come out. He told us that he had little medication to reduce the pain while the tooth was extracted, but since it was impossible to work on my teeth without anesthesia, he would give me one injection, which would be enough to keep me comfortable while he worked on me. The dentist tried to work rapidly, but there were more problems than he expected and the tooth broke as he extracted it. As the dentist continued to work, I felt a great deal of pain. I remember the dentist saying that he could not give me another injection, but that he would be finished soon so the pain would not be too bad. I do not remember much more about what happened after that and must have fainted after a while. It was a good thing that I blacked out because I could not have stood the pain much longer.

Our fears of an invasion increased after July 17, 1945. We could usually see American planes on raiding missions as tiny dots high up in the sky and sometimes heard distant explosions of bombs. We guessed that the Americans were bombing the outskirts of Shanghai, where the Japanese may have stationed troops or where they stored fuel and ammunition. We had little fear during the air raids because we assumed that the Americans, knowing that Jewish refugees were there, would not bomb the ghetto, which had nothing of military value anyway. When the air raid sirens sounded, and even during actual bombardments, clusters of refugees gathered in various viewing spots secretly cheering the American planes on after picking them out with field glasses. All of that changed after July 17. The ghetto was bombed on that day and thirty-one refugees were killed.

It was an enormous shock to all of us to have such a heavy bombardment of the ghetto when the end of the war seemed close at hand. We had noticed that a building on Seward Road, occupied by the Japanese army, had large rooftop antennas. A few Japanese soldiers frequently wandered in and out of that area, but no one paid much attention to it. That building seemed to have been the major target of the air raid and was completely demolished, and most of the destruction in the ghetto fanned out from that area. We guessed afterward that the building must have housed a Japanese military radio station.

After the all clear sirens signaled the end of the raid, my father walked along one of the badly damaged streets. He saw two legs, which seemed to belong to a European man, sticking out of the rubble near a house that must have suffered a direct hit. After helping to clear the bricks away, my father was shocked to recognize the man buried under the rubble as someone we had known very slightly. My father said that the man's throat seemed to have been cut by shrapnel.

After that bombardment the wailing of air raid sirens during the rest of that humid summer turned our perspiration into the cold sweat of fear. At the first sound of the sirens we all looked for safer places. Since there were no air raid shelters anywhere in Hongkew, or in the rest of the city, we looked for safety in the most sturdily constructed houses. In Hongkew the most massive buildings were in the huge prison, whose main entrance was directly across the street from the Ward Road Heim. The Japanese gave the refugees permission to enter some of the office buildings in the prison compound during air raids. We felt safe there because the adults reasoned that bombing hospitals or prisons was forbidden in agreements signed by most countries long before the beginning of the war. My father explained that the bombing of prisons had been forbidden in the Geneva agreements because people in jail could not flee to safer areas or move to protect themselves.

The prison compound was a block wide and six blocks long and surrounded by a high wall. Most of the buildings were four or five stories high and had been built out of massive concrete. Once the sirens started to wail for an expected raid we ran for the prison and stayed there until the all clear signal was sounded. Those who could not get to the compound before the beginning of an air raid tried to find shelter in a doorway or corner inside a building, since these seemed to be the safest spots. We had noticed that doorways often remained standing even though the rest of a house had been destroyed.

One day while we were sheltered in the Ward Road jail during an air raid I noticed a young Austrian refugee whom my parents knew slightly. He lived on a street not far from the radio station that had been wiped out in the July 17 raid. This man was standing near my mother and could not seem to remain still. I was embarrassed to realize that he was trying to slowly push himself into a doorway in the prison by gently shoving my mother away from it.

There were a lot of things on my mind during that summer. I was afraid of the bombardments and worried about my dysentery and about how little money my parents had left. But in back of my mind lurked my approaching bar mitzvah. I was to turn thirteen in November 1945 and, because the Jewish calendar differs slightly from the usual one, the date for my bar mitzvah would be about a month earlier. Even though I was a good student in the yeshiva and worked hard on the sections of the Talmud we were studying, a lot of additional preparation for my bar mitzvah was needed.

Instead of merely the last few sentences I intended to chant the whole section of the Bible scheduled to be read that Saturday in my parents' synagogue, where the bar mitzvah would be celebrated. In addition, I would also chant the excerpt from the Prophets. In the yeshiva, Rabbi Meyer Frankel taught me how to chant the notes while reading from the Torah and supervised me while I memorized them, since the Torah scrolls did not contain any notes or punctuation. Rabbi Frankel had memorized all five volumes of the Torah and the notes with which they should be chanted, so he could correct me without even glancing at the book. I also studied the notes used to chant the segment from the Prophets; the notes for these selections were the same as those for the Torah, but the chants used for each note varied slightly. Despite the different chants, studying the selection from the Prophets was much easier because it was read from a volume in which both the words and the notes appeared on the printed page.

I also intended to deliver a speech after chanting the sections from the Torah and the Prophets. My teachers in the Mirrer Yeshiva suggested that knowledgeable students often delivered a special commentary on the Torah as well. Rabbi Abraham Aaron Kreiser, who gave me individual instruction, helped me prepare both the speech and the commentary. Immersing myself in these preparations helped me escape from my worries.

In early August a one paragraph news story in the *Shanghai Jewish Chronicle* announced that American forces had exploded a new type of bomb over Hiroshima using energy from splitting the atom. A number of knowledgeable refugees said that such a bomb must have created enormous destruction and predicted that the war would soon be over. The announcement of the new bomb was followed by two or three days of severe wind, rain, and flooding. While such floods happened pretty often during the rainy season in Shanghai, the waves in the Huangpu River were rolling in so violently that the embankments along the harbor were no match for the fury of the waters. Five days later we learned that Nagasaki had been destroyed by a second atomic bomb. Shortly after that we heard that the Japanese had surrendered.

There was a great deal of jubilation at the Allied victory, but an uneasy silence quickly settled over Shanghai. News suddenly stopped flowing in, and the Japanese occupying forces mysteriously disappeared. Rumors circulated that they had withdrawn to compounds at the edge of the city, but it was difficult to be certain about exactly what was going on. For a few days it seemed as if no one was in charge of the city; the police became invisible and it was not clear that any other city departments were operating. Although some refugees crossed the ghetto borders for the first time in three years to wander all over the city, others felt it was too dangerous to leave.

Rumors soon spread through the ghetto that a large American army plane had landed at the airport and that a small tank had rolled out of the massive aircraft. We soon learned that the vehicle was called a Jeep. Shortly thereafter several Jeeps could be seen being driven around the city by a small force of U.S. Army personnel who had landed in Shanghai. They were followed in a few days by larger groups of Chinese soldiers. Now everyone was sure that the war had finally ended.

9   Holocaust

We were fortunate to have survived the war, but most refugees felt their lives had been extremely difficult, even considering the problems we had faced in prewar Shanghai. The deaths of many people in the ghetto, the diseases to which our bodies had little resistance and that could hardly be treated with the limited medicine available, the cramped and dirty living conditions, our meager diets, and the scarcity of food had made life almost unbearable. These conditions combined with our fears of Ghoya and his whims and the threat of bombardments during the war's final months made us feel lucky to have remained alive.

Throughout the war we were anxious about what might have happened to our relatives and friends in Europe. Some refugees speculated that our families must have made their way to the East to find safety behind the Russian lines. Others reasoned that they were probably having problems much like the ones we had lived through. These people felt that the Jews left in Europe may have been liberated by the advancing American or British forces in the West or by the Russians in the East. Those few refugees, like my father, who had personal experiences in German concentration camps said very little during these conversations. An anxious look often crossed Father's face when people speculated about the fates of our relatives, but even when asked directly he usually answered with something like, "Who knows?" Often I thought about how anxious my father and Mr. Solny were a couple of years before when I overheard them worry that many of our relatives might have ended up in places like Dachau. When I remembered what they had said on that day, I tried to think of something else.

Our celebrations about the Japanese surrender ended abruptly. Shortly after the war's end news that millions of Jews had been killed in German concentration camps trickled into Shanghai. We first heard of Treblinka. The *Shanghai Jewish Chronicle* printed a series of articles about how Jews had been gassed to death and then incinerated in that camp, and shudders of fear and horror rattled through the ghetto. Prayer meetings were held in all the synagogues to honor those who had perished, and my parents, like everyone else, were filled with a gnawing anxiety about the fates of their relatives in Europe. We had heard nothing from any of them since the outbreak of the war.

We then heard about the Belsen concentration camp, followed shortly thereafter by Auschwitz. Our fears deepened, even as lists of survivors were posted and published. The *Aufbau*, a Jewish newspaper from New York published in German and read by those who had been lucky enough to enter the United States, made its way to Shanghai. Every week lists of survivors and those murdered in the German extermination camps were printed. No one expressed much pleasure when news reached us that a friend or relative had survived. There were too many others in all our families whose fates were still unknown. We held our breath from week to week awaiting the arrival of each issue of the *Aufbau*.

We finally heard that my mother's sister, Malkah Jaffe, her husband, Philip, and my cousins Sigi and Max were alive and living in a displaced persons camp in Germany. I remembered that we used to visit the Jaffes almost every week in Berlin. My mother was very close to her sister. After her arrival in Berlin, and before she and my father were married, my mother had lived with the Jaffes and worked in their store. Uncle Philip was a tailor and the Jaffes sold suits, pants, jackets, and textiles. Whenever we went to see them at their home on Petersburger Strasse in Berlin we spent a lot of time in their shop.

After we learned that they had survived, I vividly remembered our last visit to the Jaffes while we were all still living in Berlin. In September 1938 Uncle Philip had received a summons to report at the Gestapo headquarters for an interrogation. We had heard that many Jews never returned from such investigations. After the summons arrived, my parents and my other aunt in Berlin, Sarah Blaufeld, and her family met at the Jaffes' house. The kids were gathered in one room while the adults met next door to discuss what the Jaffes should do. While the adults were careful to speak in whispers out of the children's earshot, even I—the youngest of the five cousins in Berlin—could see from the worried looks that something ominous was in the air. When the meeting broke up, I did not know what had been decided but we kissed and hugged all the Jaffes before leaving, as if we would not be seeing them for a very long time. My parents told me not to talk about our visit during the trolley car ride back to our apartment.

When we arrived home, I learned that Uncle Philip would not report to the Gestapo. Instead, the Jaffes were going to join the rest of my mother's family in Szendiszov, Poland. They left their apartment the next day, a Sunday afternoon, and acted as if they were visiting someone nearby. They took only the clothes they wore and the few things that could be carried without calling attention to themselves while making their way to the railroad station. They left everything in their apartment and all the goods in their shop. I remember wondering what would become of all the jackets and suits left hanging on the racks.

It was a relief to know that the Jaffes had survived. Then we learned that my cousin Sol Blaufeld was also alive, after being shuttled to seven different work camps, and was staying in another displaced persons camp in Germany. Before the war Sol and his family also lived in Berlin and we saw them quite often. After my father left for Shanghai, we spent a lot of time at the Blaufelds, and my mother urged them again and again to flee to China with us. I realized now that my mother was eager to have the Blaufelds join us so that we would have some relatives in Shanghai. Sol's parents decided to join the Jaffes in Szendiszov instead. We waited for news about the rest of the Blaufeld family but heard nothing for a long time.

After that we received horrible news. My father had one brother who had emigrated to Palestine before the war, and he was safe there. The rest of his relatives, a total of four families, had been exterminated in the camps. My father had always been a talkative and friendly man; now he rarely spoke and was often in tears. It was awful to see his grief. I was horrified that all my father's family had been killed, but I had few personal memories of them since we usually spent summers with my mother's relatives.

Then we heard the terrible news that, outside of the Jaffes and Sol Blaufeld, all of my mother's family in Poland had been killed. After that news reached us, I was often flooded with vivid memories of my dead relatives. During the day, I could usually push these images out of mind. At night my dreams were often so real that, upon waking, I was uncertain whether they had actually been killed or if it was all part of a bad dream. The doubts disappeared once I saw my mother's red-rimmed eyes and my father's gaunt face.

My mother and I spent the summer before we came to Shanghai in Szendiszov with my Uncle Aaron, who ran an egg exporting business with stores in two other Polish towns. Occasionally, we also visited my other uncle, Melech, and his wife in Katowitz, where he managed that branch of the egg business. Now I kept looking at our pictures of Uncle Aaron and his fiancée, Taube. Even though he was the younger of the two brothers, Uncle Aaron was very smart and he managed the family's business all over Poland. Whenever there was a problem of any kind, we always went to him for advice. It was Aaron who had first noticed my head tilting to the left; he had made my mother promise to have my neck examined by the best doctor she could find when we got back to Berlin. Taube was a beautiful, friendly young woman, whom I liked enormously. She lived in a town not far from Szendiszov and often came to visit Aaron, traveling on the back seat of a motorcycle driven by one of her neighbors. The family let me play on the motorcycle, safely pulled up on its kickstand, whenever she was visiting. Now that we had heard the terrible news I wondered if Aaron and Taube were together when they were killed.

I remember pretending to ride Taube's motorcycle and imitating the roar of the engine while energetically honking the horn. Many of the Polish kids passing by shot envious looks at me while muttering curses under their breath. Although I could remember only a few words of Polish now, I could clearly remember the cutting tone with which the Polish kids spat out the word *Zhid* (Jew); it felt as if they were throwing stones at me. I had often been called "dirty Jew" in Hitler's Germany, but I was shaken by the nastiness with which the Poles cursed at me during our summer visits. I was always surprised by the depth of their hatred since I regularly played with a number of the Polish boys from the town. There was a large meadow in front of the family's house in Szendiszov, and we often took turns to see who could toss things farthest into the field. Uncle Aaron always let me take the spoiled eggs from the storeroom for these contests. The family scolded me more than once when I sneaked some good eggs out of the storeroom after we had used up the rotten ones. I now realized that the Polish kids in Szendiszov played with me for only as long as I supplied them with eggs.

I remember feeling especially close with Ida, the youngest and most beautiful of my mother's five sisters. Ida used to spend more time with me than anyone else during our yearly summer stay in Poland. Although I was excited when Ida got married I never felt particularly

comfortable with her husband, Herman. Ida became pregnant shortly after her marriage and gave birth to a baby the winter before our
last visit to Szendiszov. After that she had much less time for me.
During my last visit to Poland in 1938 I realized that Ida was pregnant again. After hearing that they had all been killed, I often caught
myself wondering whether she and her two infants knew they were
about to die when they were shoved into the gas chambers.

My mother's family owned a truck that was used to transport eggs
among the three stores. I spent a lot of time with Saul, a Jewish em-
ployee who drove the truck and performed other jobs for Uncle Aaron.
He often took me along with him for short trips on the truck. Once
we left the village, he often sat me on his lap and let me handle the
truck's steering wheel. Saul made me promise not to tell anyone our
secret, that he let me "drive the truck." I remembered both of our voices
rising above the din of the engine, as we sang Polish and Yiddish songs
while the truck was roaring down the country roads. As I now thought
of Saul, I suddenly realized that my mother urged me not to speak of
him so often when we got back to Berlin so that I would not hurt my
father's feelings. Saul was killed in the gas chambers of Treblinka.

I remembered how Saul took me along one day when he had to drive
to Dembitz, where Aunt Rachel, the oldest of my mother's sisters, and
her husband ran the third of the family's stores. It was a dusty drive
on a warm summer day, and Aunt Rachel welcomed us with drinks
of cold milk and lemonade. Rachel was a kindly woman who looked
like a schoolteacher because she always squinted through heavy eye-
glasses. My cousin Shlomek (many of the cousins were named after
my grandfather from Szendiszov whose Hebrew first name was So-
lomon) was like Aunt Rachel in many ways, including his thick glasses. Shlomek and I never really got along. I remember that Shlomek
was usually the center of everyone's attention; they always said that
he was the smartest of all the cousins in the family. Shlomek seemed
to have his nose stuck in a book a lot of the time. He easily solved

puzzles, riddles, or anything else that stumped me and the rest of the cousins. I was glad that Shlomek was a little awkward physically and that I could usually beat him at most athletic games. We learned in Shanghai that Aunt Rachel, my cousin Shlomek, and his sister were killed in one of the death camps; only Rachel's husband, David Reiner, survived.

Just after the outbreak of the war my uncle Melech and his wife joined the rest of the family in Szendiszov. The village was occupied by the Germans on the second day of Rosh Hashanah in 1939. On that day the Germans backed trucks up to the synagogue, where all the Jews in town had gathered for services; all the men in the synagogue were then ordered into trucks, taken to a nearby forest, and executed. My mother's three other sisters and their families were later exterminated in Belsen. All of the other relatives in both of my parents' families, more than forty people, had been exterminated.

When the awful news dribbled in, one bit more horrible than the next, my mother grieved for weeks. In her despair, one day she asked one of my teachers in the yeshiva, "If there is a God in heaven, how could he allow the most learned, the most religious part of the Jewish community to be slaughtered like that?"

My teacher answered, "If you slap someone, you slap him in the face."

I did not understand that answer, and it did not comfort me or my parents. Many of the prayers I recited three times a day on every day of the year described God as being mighty, just, and merciful. After the news about our family in Europe reached us, it was hard for me to think of God as merciful. My confusion often turned to anger and I usually simply skipped over those words in my prayers.

During the first few months after we heard that our relatives in Europe had been killed, both of my parents were often in tears. At those times I tried to make my way out of our room as quickly as possible, fleeing into troubled prayer at the yeshiva. Perhaps there was some mistake, perhaps this uncle or this aunt had made it to safety after all?

I had never told anyone some of the things about which I was most ashamed. I remembered that during my last visit to Dembitz I had picked a fight with my cousin Shlomek and had broken his glasses while we were wrestling. I was always angry at all the attention he got and jealous because everyone considered him to be so smart. When the news that he had been killed reached us in Shanghai, I was haunted by the memory of our fight.

I also felt ashamed about my last memories of my beautiful cousin Puppe Blaufeld, who was almost four years older than I. She was also very smart and always had an answer for everything. One day, while we were all still living in Berlin, Puppe developed a blister. After overhearing conversations between my mother and Aunt Sarah, I figured out that the blister must have been on her behind. Aunt Sarah asked me to leave the room and, realizing that she and my mother would probably examine Puppe, I peeked through the keyhole to see what was going on. As they examined her, Puppe heard me behind the door. Naturally, she screamed and raged when she found me peeking through the keyhole and would not speak to me for days.

After we heard that Puppe and Shlomek had been killed in concentration camps, I could remember only these last shameful images. During those days I became a *masmid* (someone who studies constantly) and spent days and nights immersed in study and prayer at the yeshiva. I prayed to be forgiven for having acted so badly toward Puppe and Shlomek, but I was rarely able to shut these memories out of my mind. I also prayed that no one else would remember how terribly I had acted toward them.

Fortunately, preparations for my bar mitzvah helped me to push the memories of my cousins, and of all the relatives who had been killed, out of my mind. When we first started to make plans for the bar mitzvah, before we received the awful news from Europe, I was really worried about having undertaken too much. Now it was a relief to be forced to practice all the things I would have to do at the service. My parents were also relieved to occupy themselves with plans for the *kiddush* (reception) in the synagogue. They worried about how many cakes we would have to bake, now that food supplies were more readily available, where we could store them, and how much schnapps we needed to make sure that there was enough for everyone. During the week before the synagogue service our whole house seemed enveloped in the wonderful aroma of cakes.

The bar mitzvah turned out to be really exciting. A few days before that Saturday an American rabbi named Morris Gordon turned up in Shanghai. He was a chaplain in the U.S. Army and happened to be in China for a few days before being discharged from the service. On the Saturday of my bar mitzvah Rabbi Gordon found his way to Oihel Moshe.

The American rabbi's presence created enormous excitement. Having lived through the beginning of Hitler's persecution of the Jews, the Japanese ghetto, all the difficulties of the war, and—worst of all—learning about the death of so many of our relatives among the six million Jews killed by the Germans, the sight of an American rabbi in an officer's uniform of the U.S. Army was almost too much to believe. Not only was this our first contact with any American rabbi, but the very idea that a rabbi had the rank of captain and casually wore a Star of David on the collar of his uniform was deeply moving to us.

My bar mitzvah also seemed to have been a moving event for Rabbi Gordon. After I delivered a speech, read the whole portion of the Torah and a section from the Prophets, and finished the commentary on the Talmud, Rabbi Gordon asked to speak to the congregation. He began by apologizing for speaking in English and promised to talk slowly, so that those who could understand him might translate for the others. He then continued, "When I landed in Shanghai, I doubted if it would be possible to find a *minyan* (ten men needed for group prayer) for sabbath services. To my delight, not only do I find a vital synagogue here in Shanghai, but I am thrilled to participate in a bar mitzvah as deeply steeped in Jewish custom, learning, and values as one could ever have imagined anywhere on earth, much less in China. From this day on, the phrase *am yisroel chai* (the people of Israel live) will have a very special meaning to me for the rest of my life."

There were few eyes without tears in the synagogue, including those of the American rabbi, my parents, and the bar mitzvah boy.

10   Life in Postwar Shanghai

Shortly after the end of the war all of Shanghai was occupied by the Chinese forces led by Generalissimo Chiang Kai-shek, the leader of China's Kuomintang, the Nationalist party. We could see that they had been supported by the United States, since the uniforms of the Kuomintang troops looked identical to those of the American army except for their insignia. For the first time since our arrival in China all of Shanghai was ruled by the Chinese. The British did not return to control the International Settlement, nor did the French now rule their concession. The only remaining signs that sections of the city had once been run by these European nations were the English and French street names. Of course, there was now no more ghetto and we were free to wander all over Shanghai. Some of the wealthier refugees moved out of Hongkew, and many others found jobs downtown.

A few months after the end of the war the Kuomintang organized trials of several Japanese army officers who had been in charge of Shanghai's occupation. After one of these, there was a parade beginning in the jail across the street from the Ward Road Heim. A Japanese officer, who had been sentenced to death, was driven to his execution through the streets of Hongkew in an open truck. The prisoner was handcuffed, and a sign with Chinese lettering describing his wartime crimes stuck out of his collar. The Chinese screamed some of their most vicious curses at the prisoner, and many spat at him as the truck slowly passed by. The Japanese officer stood ramrod straight and seemed to smile in contempt at the abuse heaped on him.

My parents, and many other refugees, watched the officer being driven through the streets of Shanghai with mixed feelings. We could understand the anger of the Chinese people, who had been treated cruelly by the Japanese. But after hearing about the horrors of Germany's extermination of European Jews, our feelings about the Japanese, and even Ghoya and the ghetto, had changed. While no one felt grateful to Ghoya, we realized how lucky we had been that the Japanese had permitted us to settle in Shanghai. Everyone recognized that few of us would still be alive if we had remained in Europe.

Shanghai also became a center for the repatriation of those American troops who had served in China. A large warehouse directly across the street from our lane on Wayside Road was renovated for the American army and became the China Theater Repatriation Service, which we called the CTRS. A stream of American soldiers arrived at the CTRS regularly and each one stayed for a week or two while arrangements for the return home were made. I often talked with GIs walking around the streets near our lane, and every once in a while one of them invited me in to the see the movies shown almost every evening in the dining room of the CTRS.

Since there were quite a few American soldiers near our lane at all hours, a number of Chinese women could be seen standing in doorways on Wayside Road every evening. Often on my way home from evening services at the Mirrer Yeshiva I heard them approach the soldiers and whisper hoarsely, "Suckie, suckie, one dollar." Often the prostitute and soldier would then get lost in one or another alley along Wayside Road. Even though I knew that I was not supposed to pay attention to these goings on, I was fascinated by them anyway and usually came home with mixed feelings of excitement and shame.

The American soldiers were also good for business in Hongkew's bars, and our neighbor Irma seemed to return from work later and later, on those nights when she came home at all. Sometimes one of Irma's American "boyfriends" visited her in the room she shared with her parents in our house. At those times my eyes were glued to the window across from Irma's room. Every once in a while Irma would lie down and rest her head on the soldier's lap while polishing her nails or while she and the soldier were just talking and smoking cigarettes. I was always disappointed that nothing more exciting happened during these visits.

Shortly after the end of the war rations prepared for the U.S. Army but no longer needed were distributed to the refugees. We quickly learned that the "10 in 1" cartons had the tastiest rations, but these were not often available, and the "C" rations were not as good but were distributed most often. There was soon an active black market for the sale of unused rations to the Chinese. The rations posed a special problem for me. We spent a long time inspecting the contents to determine what was kosher. Obviously, bacon was not kosher and my parents immediately sold the large cans of bacon we sometimes received. Cookies in some rations were made with lard and therefore were also not kosher. I was bitterly disappointed when my teachers in the yeshiva warned me that some of the candies in the rations should not be eaten either because they had been made from unknown chemicals that might not be kosher.

After the war we, and many of the other refugees, started to contact relatives in other parts of the world. Once contact had been established we began to receive packages of used clothing and nonperishable foods from our relatives in America. We picked the packages up in the central post office, where they were inspected by the customs officers to make sure they did not contain anything on which we had to pay import duties. When we finally got the packages home, there was a lot of excitement while we tried the clothing on. Even though we were always disappointed when the clothes did not fit, my parents did not mind it all that much. They seemed happy to know that there were people in the world outside of Shanghai who cared about what was happening to us.

During the war I had noticed that my head was being pulled further and further to the right. Even though no one in the yeshiva ever made fun of me by calling me *Schiefkopf*, I was extremely unhappy about the way I looked. Now that the war was over, I kept after my parents to find a physician who could tell us what to do about my neck. We heard that Dr. Heilborn, a German surgeon, might help us. After examining me Dr. Heilborn said that a muscle on the right side of my neck had gotten stronger than the same muscle on the other side and was pulling my head in that direction. He was convinced that a simple operation, which had very little risk, would correct the problem. Because this was an unusual and interesting case, Dr. Heilborn offered to perform the surgery for free.

I urged my parents to give their permission for the operation immediately. My father seemed sympathetic, but my mother refused and would not even discuss the matter with me. My father reminded me of the frightening times during 1937 in Berlin when my mother needed surgery for the removal of gallstones. She was in a great deal of pain and in desperation finally agreed to have an operation to remove the gallstones. My mother's surgery was performed in Berlin, and a very important Nazi official happened to be a patient at the same hospital during her stay there. I could still remember even now how frightened I was whenever we saw all the important-looking German officers while visiting my mother in the hospital. There were Nazi officers near the hospital entrance, in the elevators going up to my mother's floor, in the corridors, and in the waiting room. When I was not at my mother's bedside, my father left me in the waiting room, also occupied by a number of German officers, while he and my aunt were in my mother's room.

I remembered being terrified of the German officers in their elegant uniforms bristling with medals. I tried very hard not to look at any of them and shrank into an overstuffed chair in the waiting room while staring down at the floor in order not to be noticed. Visiting officials greeted each other by raising their arm in the Nazi salute, snapping *"Heil,"* and clicking their heels. The thud of the clicking heels jolted me again and again, as I shrank more deeply into my chair. Even now in Shanghai I could still remember clearly the gleaming boots of the Nazi officers and their pistols stuck in shiny holsters. Whenever we visited my mother, it seemed that I could breathe freely only after we had left the hospital.

My father pointed out now that my mother must have been even more frightened of being a patient in that Berlin hospital than we were to visit it. He suggested that I give her some time to think about my operation, and he would also try to talk to her about it. After waiting a while I started to bother my mother again, and she finally compromised by seeking the guidance of the Amshenover Rebbe about the operation. The rebbe was a Chassidic holy man from Amshenov in Poland; he had become separated from his followers and ended up in Shanghai when the Mirrer Yeshiva arrived. My mother felt close to the rebbe because some of his followers had lived in Szendiszov.

The rebbe was a tiny man with a long white beard. He listened to our story, looked at my tilted head, and touched my back. In a soft voice and with a warm smile, he advised against the surgery, saying that it was really more important to worry about one's spiritual well-being than about one's body. My mother was triumphant and again refused to discuss the matter further. I told her that even though the Amshenover Rebbe was a holy man, he really did not know me. I felt we should get the advice of an equally saintly man, Reb Yechezkel, the *mashgiach* of the Mirrer Yeshiva, who knew me slightly in addition to being a tenant. My mother could not refuse to see Reb Yechezkel, since she also admired him.

Reb Yechezkel listened to our story and ended up agreeing with me that there seemed little reason not to correct the problem, especially since the operation seemed to be quite safe. Once my mother heard the drift of his comments she heatedly informed him of the Amshenover Rebbe's comments. I was delighted when the *mashgiach* simply shrugged off the rebbe's advice.

With Reb Yechezkel's blessing, the surgery was scheduled shortly thereafter. There were no difficulties when the operation was performed at the Jewish Hospital on Rue Pichon, in the French concession. The hospital had been founded by the Russian and Sephardic Jews in Shanghai, and several of the other patients in the room with me were Russian, as were most of the nurses. I was hospitalized for two weeks and was happy that my head was now as straight as that of everyone else.

After the operation our attention turned to leaving China. Even though we had been lucky to end up in Shanghai, no one wished to stay here for good but few refugees wanted to return to Europe. Some Zionists talked about settling in Palestine, but we read that the British were stopping ships filled with concentration camp survivors and sending them back to Europe. We realized that the chances of landing safely in Palestine after leaving Shanghai could not be very good, and no one wanted to be returned to Shanghai if they were caught by the British. Most refugees tried to establish contact with relatives in the United States, Canada, Australia, or South America, hoping to find some place to establish a new home.

My parents had applied to enter the United States from Germany in 1935 and our names were then added to the immigration waiting list. When we arrived in Shanghai before the war, the American consul there told us that it would be a long time before our number on the waiting list was reached. Now, after the war, we were told pretty much the same thing, since the U.S. immigration laws did not change after the war. New laws did make it easier for survivors of the concentration camps, who were now living in displaced persons camps in Germany, to enter the United States but these laws did not apply to us in China.

Surprisingly, it was quite easy for me to get a visa to the United States providing I left without my parents. I had been born in Berlin, and the yearly quota of German-born immigrants was much larger than the quota for most of the Eastern European countries combined. Of course my parents were not eager to have me go to the United States alone after just turning thirteen, and I was frightened of traveling so far away from them by myself. Other refugees who were born in Germany began to make plans to leave for the United States, while we worried about where our family would finally find a new home. My parents contacted some relatives in Sydney, who were ready to help us move there, and we began talking about settling in Australia.

Most of the people from the yeshiva had also been born in Eastern Europe and thus could not get regular immigration visas for the United States either. We learned that members of the yeshivas could get student visas, making it possible for them to settle in America while they were studying the Talmud. During the next few months the yeshiva students received invitations from American yeshivas. The Mirrer Yeshiva also arranged for me, and the other students who had joined the school in Shanghai, to get such invitations. One day I received an official-looking letter from the United States inviting me to be a student at the Yeshiva Chaim Berlin in New York. The letter said that the yeshiva would pay for my transportation to New York and offered me a scholarship so that my tuition, room, and board would be free. Since I was only fourteen, I was not ready to strike out for the United States by myself on a student visa without knowing where my parents would end up.

As many of the refugees prepared to leave Shanghai we began to worry about a new problem. A thorough medical examination complete with X-rays was required before an American visa could be issued. We learned that the examination was designed to make certain that prospective immigrants were not suffering from various infectious diseases, such as tuberculosis and trachoma. We soon heard that it was possible for the X-rays to show signs of encapsulated tuberculosis even though the person had no symptoms of the disease. Since tuberculosis was widespread in Shanghai, and everyone was exposed to it at one time or another, making arrangements for taking the X-rays became quite anxiety-arousing.

By mid-1947 the yeshivas left Shanghai for the United States. Before the students and instructors left, we had agreed that I would rejoin the yeshiva after my parents had arrived in the United States, even though the quota system would likely not change and no one knew when or if my parents would get to the United States. On the day when my teachers and the senior students of the Mirrer Yeshiva left for America, I felt lost and very much alone when I stood on the shore and watched their ship gradually pull away to start its journey for the United States.

11 Going to Work

*O*nce the Mirrer Yeshiva had left Shanghai I did not know what to do with myself. After I joined the yeshiva all my time was spent there and most of the people with whom I was in contact were also connected with it. Now that the yeshiva was gone, my parents urged me to go back to the Kadoorie school. I refused to do that. It would be extremely embarrassing to return to SJYA—almost an admission that it had been a mistake to leave in the first place. While I did not tell anyone, I was also worried that studying at SJYA would be difficult for me after four years away from the school, especially since I had so many problems before leaving. Being considered a good student in the yeshiva made me feel better about myself as a student, but I had no idea if I would be equally capable in a regular school.

I also felt that I now had little in common with the students at SJYA. It seemed to me that while I had been struggling with difficult Talmudic problems dealing with civil and religious laws, the kids at SJYA were concerned with unimportant matters and childish games. I could not imagine going back to school and having to worry about the endless rules of English grammar or many of the other subjects that seemed silly to me now. I did not admit to anyone that the only thing about the Kadoorie school that interested me was having a chance to get to know some of the pretty girls whom I had secretly watched around Hongkew. I had heard that many boys of my age who remained in the Kadoorie school had learned to dance and were talking about taking their girlfriends out on dates. In the yeshiva my friends and I had little contact with girls of our own age, though we certainly thought about them a lot. I felt awkward around girls and knew that I would be clumsy if I tried to dance. In any event, it was clear to me that being occupied with such problems was childish. I kept hoping that some of the pretty girls from SJYA would be impressed by the really important and difficult problems with which I had been struggling in the yeshiva and could not understand why none of them seemed to care much about that.

My parents and I finally decided that it would be best to have me register in a business school run by one of the refugees so that I could pick up some typing and office skills. After that I found a job in a refugee-owned company with an office in downtown Shanghai. My job was to do some clerical work, run errands, and help out in the stockroom. The company traded in textiles and ready-made clothes imported from the United States and also had textiles manufactured in local mills that were sold to businesses and tailors in Shanghai. A group of peddlers sold the company's textile goods door to door, just as my father had done in Berlin. All of the peddlers were refugees, and I knew many of them from the ghetto. The peddlers came to the stockroom in the morning to pick up their goods, paid for anything they sold during the day when they got back in the evening, and returned the unsold goods.

Many of my friends from the yeshiva, who had also remained in Shanghai, found other jobs with which to occupy themselves. I was glad that my work kept me busy, but wondered when I would rejoin the yeshiva and when my parents would be able to get visas so that we could finally leave China.

I got to know the peddlers pretty well. These men claimed to know everything about everyone in the ghetto and told funny stories, knew lots of dirty jokes, and traded rumors about refugees and the people they had dealt with during the day. I finally met some Russian Jews and many other refugees whom I had never known in the tight little world of the yeshiva.

For the first time I began to hear a great deal of anger and resentment at the yeshivas. It was easy not to pay too much attention to anything the peddlers said, since they always exaggerated everything, but many other refugees were also extremely critical of my former teachers. It had been clear to us that the yeshivas were receiving money from the United States throughout the war. Rumors now circulated that the money had come to Shanghai through neutral Switzerland; every person in the yeshiva community was supposed to have received thirty American dollars every month throughout the war, though no one could be sure of the exact amount. That was a lot of money even after the war; it was a fortune during the years in the ghetto. While those of us who left SJYA to study the Talmud full-time did receive some support from the yeshiva, it was never more than four or five dollars a month and seemed to be a small part of the money the yeshivas were supposed to have received for us from America.

I did not know what to do or say when the peddlers and other refugees imitated the way some yeshiva students showed off their new clothes to each other on high holidays during the war years. Others mimicked overheard conversations among people connected with the yeshivas about buying meat, butter, cream, or other foods that only they could afford. During the difficult war years most of the Jewish refugees, whether they were Orthodox, Conservative, Reform, or not at all religious, often became ill with painful, and sometimes deadly, diseases because they did not have enough food. Many refugees were now saying that the people in the yeshivas were hypocrites who hid their greed with religion, yet did not care if the other Jews in the ghetto lived or died. People wondered if we would have needed the three cemeteries, which were now almost filled with Jewish refugees who had died in Shanghai, if we had had a little more food during the war.

It was confusing to hear how angry people were at the yeshivas, and I sometimes felt ashamed to have joined one. I tried not to listen to such talk but could not avoid hearing the condemnation. Even though I said nothing during these conversations I was flooded with mixed feelings. I felt angry, sometimes at the people spreading the rumors, at other times at the yeshivas, and often at both. I also became confused about religion and my belief in God. My faith was shaken when the news first reached us in Shanghai about the extermination of my aunts, uncles, cousins, and the six million other Jews. Now it became even more difficult to remain religious when I heard what was being said about the people I had admired so much.

The criticisms of the yeshivas haunted me when I was alone. Sometimes I felt that I now couldn't believe in anything and wanted to stop practicing the laws by which Orthodox Jews live. At other times I felt that there must be some explanation for the way the yeshivas had acted that I just could not figure out. My teachers had often taught us about how the faith of ancient Jewish sages was tested during their lives. At times I felt that this was my time of trial, and at other times I made fun of myself for holding on to a faith learned from people who were so hypocritical. What was most confusing was that I could not think of being Jewish without being Orthodox, and I was nothing if not Jewish.

I felt much too ashamed to discuss my confusion with anyone, including my parents, and spent a lot of time by myself trying to sort out these painful feelings and confusing ideas. Externally, it must have seemed to most people that I had not changed at all. I continued to pray three times a day, did not eat anything that was not kosher, attended services every Saturday at Oihel Moshe, and obeyed all the restrictions on the sabbath. During many prayer services I felt bewildered, and my feelings sometimes changed completely every few minutes. One moment I felt an unquestioning faith in God but the next I was overcome with anger and bitter cynicism at the hypocrisy of the people in the Mirrer Yeshiva.

Since I spent so much time by myself trying to deal with these problems I looked forward to the distractions in the office where I worked. Shortly after the war the Kuomintang government replaced the currency that had been issued by the Japanese. Within a year the new currency had lost most of its value and many of the refugees compared the situation with the inflation that they had lived through after the end of World War I in Germany. The official exchange rate, set by the Chinese government, was thirty-five hundred yuan for one U.S. dollar. The banks paid that rate for any money officially sent to banks in Shanghai from the United States. On the black market, however, the price for American money climbed almost daily. Within a year after the end of the war U.S. dollars were traded on the black market for almost ten times more than the official rate paid by the banks. The Chinese government issued colorful and crisp new bills frequently. Generally, one unit of the new currency was declared to be worth some large number of the old bills, and the process was repeated several times each year.

The value of Chinese money fell daily, and it got to the point that a package of paper bills was needed to buy anything of value; the packages of money got to be so huge that they had to be carried around in sacks. It became difficult to manage the piles of bank notes tied up with string to form packets almost a foot high. The wax seal of a company or bank was stamped on each packet of money at the spot where the strings were tied, so that the wax would have to be broken in order to extract any money from the packet. If anyone recognized the seal on top of a batch of money, the bills in the packet were never counted; the time needed to count the money cost more than the stacks of bills were worth.

It was illegal, just as it had been during the war, to own U.S. dollars, to buy and sell anything with them, or to trade in dollars. Despite that, everyone figured the true cost of anything in American dollars. During this period, I often acted as a messenger for my bosses by carrying bunches of checks and cash to and from money changers. One day I was frightened and excited when my boss asked me to carry an enormous sum, fifty-five thousand American dollars in cash and checks, to the office of people who were black market dealers in U.S. currency. I was also often asked to hide the U.S. currency in some of the jackets and coats in the stockroom in case the police raided us. My employers thought that no one would guess that a teenager would carry that much money around or know where it was hidden. Because of these new duties, my salary had gone up to nine American dollars a week.

I was paid in American money and then turned my salary over to my parents, who gave me a little pocket money to go to the movies and take the streetcar to my job. Even in postwar Shanghai nine dollars was a lot of money, and we were able to live on it for the week and still had some money left to save. The Chinese employees were paid in yuan; they usually took time off on paydays to buy big sacks of rice and other durable goods before the prices went up further.

My new duties at work were exciting but frightening. Since merely possessing American money was illegal, being a messenger for money trading was a much more serious offense. I worried about what would happen if the police ever caught me. My bosses told me that there was little risk of being caught, and that even if it should happen it would be easy to get me off by bribing the right people. There were rumors that a number of businessmen had been freed in just that way. When I told my parents of my fears they asked my employer to transfer me to other tasks. I was sent to work in a fur store on Avenue Joffre, the main street of the former French concession, in which the company rented a counter to sell textiles retail. I knew how much to charge for each type of material in American dollars, and my major job was to call the money changer's office every few hours to adjust the prices in Chinese currency according to the present rate.

My duties in the store were light. A Chinese man showed the materials to customers; he also changed the prices we posted in the store window. The inflation got to be so bad, however, that we stopped posting prices because they had to be changed several times each day. Instead, the Chinese clerk checked with me before quoting a price for anything. Because there was little work I often took time off from the store to attend services at the new synagogue on those Jewish holidays, such as Chanukah and Purim, when work was permitted.

The yeshiva used to take up most of my time, so now I found myself with little to do. Many American films, some made during the war but new to us, were being shown in Shanghai, and I spent many evenings at the theaters. The three theaters showing American movies in Hongkew had such ancient projectors that it was often difficult to understand what the actors said. I preferred traveling to some of the downtown theaters, where the sound was much clearer, to see the newer films or even some of the others before they came to Hongkew.

I didn't feel much like reading while I was trying to sort out my feelings about the yeshiva. I began to hang around with some of the athletic clubs in Hongkew. I took an interest in boxing and spent time with a small group of refugees who trained for boxing meets against American soldiers and others. All the refugees followed the news of those fights very closely and we attended as many of them as we could afford. Successful boxers, like Alfred "Laco" Kohn, were great heroes among the refugees. My father knew the trainer of the boxers, Max Buchsbaum, from Berlin. Buchsbaum had a cauliflower ear from the days when he competed as a fighter. My father got Buchsbaum to let me exercise with the boxers. I particularly enjoyed using the different punching bags and even sparred occasionally with some of the boxers during training workouts. Buchsbaum kept urging me to participate in one of the boxing matches, but I always refused. Even though I was troubled about the years I had spent in the yeshiva, I felt it was not fitting for a former yeshiva student to become a boxer.

I also spent a lot of time following the news about the battle for independence being fought by the Jews in Palestine. I strongly supported the Zionist goal of forming a Jewish homeland and considered joining one of the Zionist groups in Shanghai. I attended one meeting of the Betar, a militant Zionist group supporting the most extreme Jewish resistance bands fighting in Palestine, such as the Irgun and Stern bands. We were proud of the way the Jews in Palestine fought against the British, and most refugees felt that it was high time that Jews took up arms against those persecuting them. There was a militaristic atmosphere at the Betar meeting; the khaki uniforms of the members were accompanied by marching, saluting, stomping of feet, and clicking of heels. Even though they saluted the Zionist flag with the Star of David, I was uncomfortable at the meeting; in my mind's eye I saw the Betar members as a Jewish Hitler Jugend. I rapidly left the meeting and never returned for another one. I discovered that I could not get interested in joining any of the other, less extreme Zionist groups in Shanghai.

There was a great deal of anger among the refugees at the British for refusing to allow survivors of the concentration camps to settle in Palestine. We remembered how the British had forbidden arriving refugees to settle in "their" International Settlement before World War II and were overjoyed when the state of Israel was finally established. Although I joined in the many celebrations in honor of the new state, proudly sang "Hatikvah"—the new Israeli national anthem—and joyfully danced the horah, I still could not bring myself to join any of the Zionist groups in Shanghai.

12   *Leaving Shanghai*

*I*n 1948 we and the other refugees still in Shanghai started fretting about a new problem. It was clear that Generalissimo Chiang Kai-shek's Kuomintang forces were losing their long struggle with the Chinese Communist forces. In addition to the *Shanghai Echo,* the new name for the *Shanghai Jewish Chronicle,* there were two daily English-language newspapers published in the city. All the papers indicated that the Chinese Communist armies led by Mao Tse-tung were advancing steadily, and we began to worry that they would soon reach Shanghai. After living through Hitler and the Japanese ghetto, no one wanted to be trapped again in Shanghai. We worried that Mao's forces might be just as unfriendly to us as the Japanese had been or that they might make it impossible for anyone to leave China.

The Chinese people were obviously getting tired of the Kuomintang. At my job I saw many examples of the people's unhappiness with the Nationalist government. The inflation got worse almost every day. One American dollar was now worth around seven hundred thousand Chinese yuan, and the value of the Chinese money was dropping daily. Merchants were complaining that it was impossible to conduct business because when anything was sold it cost more money to buy the same materials again or to manufacture them. Since it was so difficult to sell anything because of the inflation, my bosses, like many other businessmen, had become even more actively involved in money changing on the black market, the only remaining profitable business. They sold American dollars for short periods of time, often only a day or two, to drive the price of dollars down slightly and then bought the American money back before the price went up again. At the end of any week, the American currency was always more valuable than it had been at the beginning of the week.

In addition to the extreme inflation, people were losing confidence in the Kuomintang because the soldiers were frightening the population. On my trip to work on Avenue Joffre I regularly saw Chinese soldiers boarding streetcars with their pistols loosely holstered. They often acted in a threatening manner and, if all the seats were taken, the soldiers forced sitting passengers to surrender their seats. Kuomintang soldiers also forced their way into movie theaters without buying tickets and picked up food and fruits from stores and street stands without paying for them. People guessed that these soldiers were so bad-tempered because they had recently returned from the front, where the Nationalist troops were being beaten by the Communists. The Chinese all over Shanghai avoided contact with the troops whenever possible, and we guessed that people in the rest of China must be getting just as tired of these undisciplined troops as we were. If the Chinese people were so frightened of the army that was supposed to protect them, we guessed that it would not be long before the Communists won their long war with the Kuomintang and occupied Shanghai.

This new danger made my parents think again about letting me go to the United States by myself. It was clear to me that I was wasting time in Shanghai. I did not want to go back to the Kadoorie school, but I was not sure about what I would do once I got to the United States. I knew that the Mirrer Yeshiva had found quarters in Brooklyn but was pretty sure that I did not want to rejoin them. I thought of either going back to regular school in the United States or perhaps studying at some other American yeshiva. I had heard that yeshiva students in the United States, unlike those in Europe or Shanghai, spent half their time studying the Talmud and worked on regular school subjects for the rest of the day. I liked the idea of dividing my time that way. I had not studied at a regular school for six years now and was worried about how well I would do when I tried to learn anything other than the Talmud.

I had been urging my parents to let me travel to the United States for some time. They kept telling me that at fifteen I was much too young to settle in America by myself, especially without knowing if they would ever be able to follow me there. I pretended to be quite certain about wanting to leave for the United States by myself and kept my anxiety about being on my own a secret from everyone. Whenever I worried about what might happen to me, I pushed the fears out of my mind so that no one would guess my feelings.

My aunt Malkah Jaffe and her whole family had moved to the United States and now lived in New York. The Jaffes had survived by making their way behind the lines of the Russian army, who shipped them to Siberia, where they remained during the war. After the Germans were defeated they traveled back to the family's home in Szendiszov and found that no one else in the family had survived. The Jaffes then ended up in a displaced persons camp in Germany and finally emigrated to the United States. Sol Blaufeld was living in Washington, D.C., where he had some cousins from his father's side of the family.

Since I would have someone to turn to in an emergency, my parents now felt that it would be safe for me to move to America by myself. Because the advances of the Communist forces seemed to be a more immediate and more serious threat than the risk of sending me to the United States by myself, my parents reluctantly agreed to let me leave Shanghai. We decided that I would apply for regular immigration papers on the German quota, since my parents' chances of eventually joining me in the United States were much better if I had a regular immigration visa than student papers. I agreed with that, especially since I did not want to be obligated to study in a yeshiva.

In August 1948, three months before my sixteenth birthday, I boarded the SS *General Gordon* to begin the journey to the United States. I tried to appear confident and relaxed while waving farewell to my parents on the dock as the ship slowly began to pull away from the shore. I did not tell anyone that I was anxious about how long it would be before I would see them again.

I spent a lot of time by myself on that voyage. One of my favorite haunts was a dimly lit corner near the ship's stern. Many hours passed while I stared at the spectacular sky, which seemed alive with its infinite display of stars. Or I gazed at the ocean and listened to the rushing of the endless waves crashing against the hull of the ship—always changing yet always the same.

The *General Gordon* was used as a troop carrier during World War II and had been slightly modified for civilian travel. The huge dormitories with four and five canvas bunks on top of each other had remained unchanged, except that only two of the five bunks were now in use—providing a little more space to the passengers sleeping on the upper and lower cots. The mess hall routine during meals was very similar to what it must have been during the *General Gordon's* service as a troop carrier. Passengers lined up for meals, which were ladled out by the cooks onto U.S. Navy style trays, with pre-pressed spaces for the different foods.

Meals were a problem for me aboard ship since I ate only kosher food and the ship did not serve such meals. Even though my faith was quite shaky, I continued to maintain most of the rituals of an observant Orthodox Jew. I ate milk, cold cereal, ice cream, and fruits from the ship's menu, but no meats or other cooked foods. I also did not eat the baked goods because we had heard they contained lard. My parents had packed me a carton of foods that would not spoil during the two-week voyage, such as several kosher smoked salamis, some matzo, as well as tins of sardines, tuna, and other canned goods. Ironically enough, most of the food had originally been shipped to us from the United States. When the mess hall staff members learned of my food restrictions, they were nice enough to give me extra fruit, milk, and whatever other foods I could eat. I generally feasted on my own provisions while the others lined up for lunch and dinner.

I also continued to pray three times each day, including wearing the phylacteries on my forehead and left arm for the morning prayer. Some of the sailors and the few non-Jewish passengers aboard ship who happened to see me during morning prayers looked at me quite strangely. But there were enough other refugees aboard who understood these customs so that it never became much of a problem.

The trip on the *General Gordon* took a decided upturn for me after we made our first stop in Japan. About a thousand Japanese girls and young women, also traveling without their parents, boarded the ship in Yokohama. The new passengers had all been born in the United States, and their families had returned to Japan before the outbreak of the war in the Pacific. As native Americans, they were entitled to return to the country of their birth rather than continue to live in Japan. Young men were probably not eligible for such repatriation because they had served in the Japanese army during the war.

Some of the Japanese girls aboard ship spoke little English, having been taken back to Japan when they were young, but a lot of the others could translate for them so that communication between most of us could easily be arranged. One attractive young woman interpreted for me while I was talking with two sisters who had lived in Hiroshima and had survived the dropping of the first atomic bomb. They told me that on the day the atomic bomb was dropped their classes happened to be on a school trip out of the city. The students were having a picnic on the outskirts of Hiroshima when they saw the fireball and mushroom cloud made by the atomic bomb. Their parents were killed by the explosion, and the two sisters never went back to see what had happened to their former house. When I asked why they had not returned, the older sister replied, "There were no streets."

The companionship of so many young people in pretty similar situations to mine made the two-week trip pass quickly. In San Francisco staff from the American Jewish Joint Committee—an organization assisting new immigrants—put me up for a few days before arranging for my train trip to New York. After being afraid of eating fresh fruit for most of our stay in China, I found the wonderful California grapes and the incredible variety of other fresh fruits irresistible. It did not seem possible to consume as much fruit as I did during my few days in San Francisco. It was a relief to my digestive system when I left California for the cross-country trip to the East Coast.

During the long train trip to New York saying prayers three times each day was pretty embarrassing. It was especially awkward to put the phylacteries on my forehead and left arm for the morning prayer since no one seemed familiar with that custom. I generally tried to rush through the prayers rapidly in the least conspicuous vacant corner of the coach to avoid the staring of other passengers.

I spent quite a lot of time on the long trip with returning GIs. The continual noise of the train's wheels made it difficult to sleep. During stops, many of us left the coach for a few minutes to stretch our legs by walking along the platform or strolling into the local station. Two of the returning servicemen were black, and I was surprised that neither one wanted to get off the train when we pulled into Albuquerque, New Mexico. I walked into the station by myself and was stunned to see an illuminated fluorescent sign over one of the men's toilets that read Colored Men. I quickly returned to the train and felt that I could not face the black soldiers. Of course I had read about discrimination against blacks—though I had never come up against it firsthand. I mumbled something about being tired and returned to my seat for a long, sleepless night filled by recurring images of other signs saying Jews Forbidden or No Jews Allowed.

When my train finally pulled into Pennsylvania Station in New York

City I was reunited with the Jaffe family and with Sol Blaufeld. We had a lot of catching up to do and shared our sorrow in recalling the many relatives we would never see again. After the first few days in New York the American Jewish Joint Committee arranged for me to live in the Hebrew National Orphan Home in Yonkers, just north of New York City. Mr. Herbert, the social worker assigned to my case, told me that my stay in the orphan home was temporary, until he and I could make more permanent plans.

I made frequent weekend visits to the Jaffes, who lived in the Williamsburgh section of Brooklyn, and rapidly learned to negotiate the two and a half hour commute by bus and several subway lines from Westchester County. On one of these trips I was accompanied by Leonard, who also lived at the orphan home and was going to see his family. We were sitting next to a heavyset police officer on a Yonkers bus and asked our neighbor, who spoke with a noticeable Italian accent, something about a particular stop. After giving us the information, the policeman asked, "Are you guys from the kike orphan home in Yonkers?"

I had never heard that particular term before and asked politely, "Pardon me, I don't understand what you mean." As soon as the words were out I noticed Leonard's flushed face as well as the squirming discomfort of the policeman and immediately understood that *kike* was no compliment. Without even thinking about it, I lectured the officer about using that insulting term. After getting the derogatory term for Italians from Leonard, I ended my tirade by asking, "How would you like me to call you a wop?"

The policeman said, "Come on kid, take it easy. I didn't mean nothin' by it," before getting off the bus at the next stop. Leonard was surprised by my reaction and told me to be more careful, pointing out that the officer could have made a lot of trouble for me. Actually, my impulsive outburst had also been a surprise to me. Nevertheless, on the rest of that trip to Brooklyn I was flushed with excitement and pretty pleased with myself.

I had heard that the Mirrer Yeshiva was functioning again in Brooklyn. I knew that I should visit my former teachers and classmates but kept putting it off. Finally during one of the trips to see my family in Brooklyn I decided to visit the yeshiva. Even before entering the main auditorium I heard the familiar hum of students working on the Talmud. I saw many of the people I knew from Shanghai and even a couple of students who had studied with me in the small yeshiva. As usual, they were hunched over their study stands while working on a selection from the Talmud. Reb Chaskell was in his customary place at the head of the auditorium. He was held in such awe that, while I was in the yeshiva, it was rare for anyone to approach him during the study sessions. I walked up to Reb Chaskell and told him that I had come to convey regards from my parents. He nodded, smiled at me in his kindly manner, and looking at me closely remarked, "You've changed from the time you were with us in Shanghai."

I had not realized that my different attitude could be seen so easily and said that having arrived very recently I wanted to take some time to catch up on my English studies. He nodded, "Whenever you are ready, you are welcome to return." Reb Chaskell then asked me to give his regards to my parents, and I took my leave.

After speaking to a few of the students I had known in Shanghai I left the yeshiva to return to the Jaffes' apartment. While walking toward the subway I suddenly realized that I had reached a firm decision not to return to the Mirrer Yeshiva, without having really been aware of it. When I first walked into the building I had the strange feeling of being an outsider in the place that had been my second home for such a long time. I felt a sense of relief that this difficult visit was over and was happy with my decision not to resume the life of a yeshiva student.

After six months in Yonkers the American Jewish Joint Committee arranged for me to live with a family in Brooklyn. When I enrolled in the local school, New Utrecht High School, the principal did not quite know where I belonged since there were no formal records of my studies in the yeshiva. He talked with me for a while, was surprised and interested when I told him about having studied in the yeshiva, and decided to place me where I belonged chronologically—the sixth term of high school. He asked me to return if things didn't work out, because it would be easy to make a change. I studied all my subjects conscientiously, fearing that my long absence from regular school might make the work hard for me. Fortunately, only algebra presented special difficulties, since I had little background for it. However, these problems were not serious enough to prevent me from working in a vegetable store for twenty hours each week after school to earn my own pocket money.

I was in constant touch with my parents through the mail and shared their worries about the worsening situation in Shanghai. In the fall and winter of 1948–49 the Chinese Communist "liberation" armies were advancing daily and capturing most of China, and the inflation was worsening every day. When I left Shanghai in August 1948 the black market exchange rate was twelve million Chinese yuan for a single American dollar; ten months later the rate was one hundred twenty million per dollar. These developments were alarming for my parents and the other Jews still stuck in Shanghai. It seemed sad that my parents' difficulties in getting a visa to enter America were identical to those they had in Germany before the war. Nevertheless, they decided to wait in Shanghai in the hope that something would happen to reunite our family in the United States.

In January 1949 many of the Jews from Shanghai were moved to Italy by an international refugee organization. Their voyage was long and tortuous, since the Egyptian government denied the ships filled with Jewish refugees permission to sail through the Suez Canal. The ships retraced my father's long journey around the African continent, arriving in Naples after being at sea for almost seven weeks.

The closing of the canal to the convoy from Shanghai was not unexpected. Two years earlier some refugees decided to return to their native country, since after a lifetime of work they were now entitled to collect pensions in their prewar homes. The ships carrying these refugees back to Europe were detained some distance before approaching the canal zone and were permitted through the canal only at night. Passengers were forbidden on deck, less they jumped ship and made their way to Palestine on foot. These refugees watched from their tiny cabin portholes as the ship steamed through what was supposed to be an international waterway on their way back to Europe. It was depressing to realize that the Jewish passengers had been free to wander about the ship when they originally fled to China but now, after the defeat of Germany, they were locked into their cabins until they had cleared the canal zone.

While some refugees from Shanghai did return to Europe, the majority had a different destination. The new state of Israel chartered several tiny vessels that made their way to Shanghai and steamed into the harbor with Israeli flags fluttering from their masts. All the Jewish residents of Shanghai were welcome to board these ships without needing to pay for tickets, and they were welcomed again when they arrived in Israel, their new homeland. No Jew needed a visa.

My parents thought of going to Israel but wrote to me before the ships arrived that they had decided to take their chances of being admitted to the United States because I was already there. A change in the immigration laws had been proposed in Congress to make it possible for them to come to the United States. After the vessels chartered by Israel left, my parents wrote that they had been tempted to change their plans at the last minute and board one of the ships. The sight of these tiny chartered ships flying the Star of David gave them so much hope for the future of the Jewish nation that they considered settling there. I was relieved when my parents finally received their visas for the United States. Our family was reunited in New York in May 1949, one month before Mao Tse-tung's armies occupied Shanghai.

We heard from friends still in China that the Communist armies entered Shanghai in an orderly manner. The remaining refugees wrote that both they and the Chinese were relieved to be free of the plundering Kuomintang forces. Typically, the Communists added the word *liberation* to the name of each of the armies entering the city, such as the Seventh "Liberation" Army. The English-language newspapers in Shanghai always printed *liberation* with quotation marks. One of the papers, the *Shanghai Evening Post,* continued publication after the city was captured by the Communists. The American editor of the paper, after comparing the correct behavior of the disciplined Communist soldiers to that of the departed Kuomintang army, wrote that he saw no reason to continue to put the word *liberation* in quotation marks and removed the quotes after that. These rosy feelings did not continue, and the newspaper was closed by the Communist authorities six months later.

About one thousand refugees remained in Communist-run Shanghai for almost another year while waiting for visas to join relatives abroad. As the Communist government imposed numerous restrictions, the remaining Jews became more desperate to leave. An arrangement was finally made for the last European Jews to receive transit visas to the United States, which enabled them to embark for San Francisco. These refugees from Hitler's Germany and Communist China were then transported across the United States in locked railroad cars, to prevent them from fleeing from the train and entering the United States illegally. When they reached New York, the refugees were put aboard a ship headed back to Europe. There, some of the former Shanghaiers continued their journey to Israel and others returned to the countries of their birth. As American immigration laws were modified, many of these former Shanghai refugees eventually emigrated to the United States.

My parents and I were sworn in as American citizens in 1955. It made us feel a little safer to became citizens of a powerful country like the United States after being stateless for so many years, when we felt that no nation cared whether we lived or died. Even though we were not planning to travel abroad, it was comforting to know that we could now get a passport and were free to travel almost anywhere in the world.

We also celebrated because becoming citizens made it possible to take back our rightful surname. Since 1935 we had been forced to use Windstrauch as our family name. As was customary among Orthodox Jews in Galicia, the part of Poland where my parents were born, my grandparents had a religious wedding in the synagogue but did not have a separate civil wedding ceremony. Poland did not recognize such weddings unless a great deal of money was paid, and Germany, after the Nuremberg laws of 1935, followed the Polish lead. The children of these unions were declared to be illegitimate and forced to assume the mother's surname. I had never liked Windstrauch because it sounded so German, and it also gave kids a chance to tease me by calling me "Windy." It felt wonderful to have our rightful family name restored in our new country.

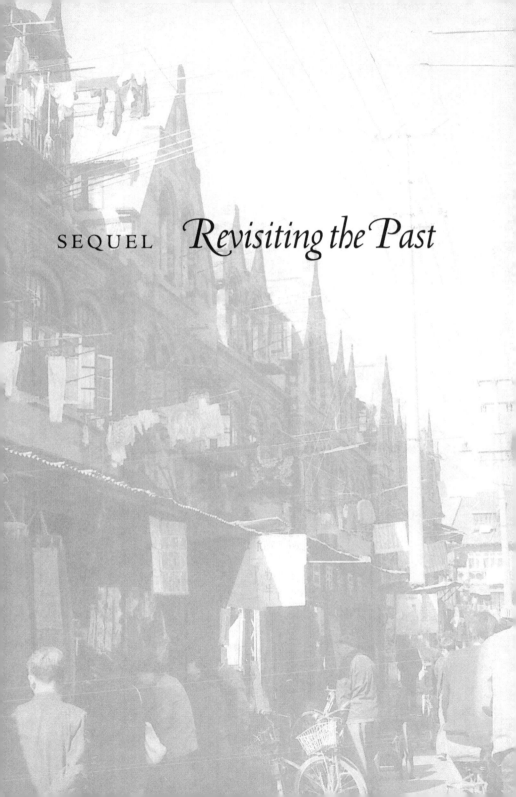

SEQUEL *Revisiting the Past*

13 Revived Childhood Memories

*A*fter settling in America I finished high school, worked my way through college, completed a master's degree in school psychology at the City College of New York, and then finished a doctorate in clinical psychology at Columbia University. Eventually I became more interested in research and teaching in educational psychology than in clinical work and ended up on the faculty of my undergraduate alma mater. I attained some visibility in the field and was elected president of both the Northeastern Educational Research Association and the Division of Educational Psychology of the American Psychological Association. Partially as a result of these activities, I was invited to give a series of lectures at the Shanghai Institute of Education in the fall of 1988.

A year earlier during a trip to Israel, I was vividly reminded of my years in Shanghai. After speaking at an international meeting in Jerusalem, my wife and I visited the Museum of the Diaspora in Tel Aviv. In the lobby of the museum we noticed an announcement for photographs and memorabilia dealing with Jews in China. We assumed that the exhibit focused on the history of a Jewish community in Kaifeng Fu that existed over three hundred years ago and had all but disappeared by the twentieth century. As we got close enough to see some of the photographs I realized that the exhibit featured our refugee community in Shanghai. While examining some of the photographs I came across a shot of a gym class at the Kadoorie school led by Leo Meyer and was stunned to recognize myself in the first row. My wife, who had seen pictures of me taken at about the same time, also recognized me and kept repeating excitedly, "That's you, Sig, that's a picture of you." I had never seen that photograph before and, with tear-filled eyes and choked throat, could only nod that indeed it was a picture of me.

After recovering from this surprise we found an archivist so that we could purchase a copy of the photo. The archivist, a friendly but down-to-earth Israeli, told me that it was not rare for visitors to find some record of their lives in the museum. When I showed her the photo of the gym class she examined it carefully, looked at me closely, smiled, and said, "You know, it really doesn't look that much like you."

By now I had regained enough of my composure to smile as well and say, "Well, I've changed a bit in the more than forty years since that picture was taken."

Finding my picture in the museum primed me for a return visit to China. I was proud when President Jimmy Carter appointed Michael Blumenthal, a member of our refugee community during the war, as secretary of the treasury. The appointment was a prime subject during the reunion of former refugees in San Francisco that year. The televised coverage of Blumenthal's visit to Hongkew, during an official trip to China, also whetted my appetite to revisit Shanghai even though I was also hesitant about such a trip. I was recuperating from an accident that left me with a ripped Achilles tendon in my left leg and a torn rotator cuff in my left shoulder. These orthopedic problems made me uneasy about the physical demands and reduced comforts a trip to China would involve. My physicians were also concerned about my ability to continue physiotherapy exercises in China and about the availability of adequate medical assistance, should it be required, during the trip.

A few years earlier I was equally hesitant about accepting a similar invitation to visit a university in Germany, but that reluctance had nothing to do with medical problems. Nevertheless, I eventually was able to put the past behind me and visited Berlin twice to speak at an international meeting and at a university. While dates for the Shanghai trip were being arranged I was contacted by the staff of the United States Holocaust Memorial Museum in Washington, D.C., who asked me to tape-record my memories of Kristallnacht. Of course, Kristallnacht also persuaded my father to flee to Belgium, which eventually led to our escape to Shanghai. The museum was collecting memories of that day to provide a database for Holocaust scholars. Transcribed excerpts of my recording were published in Washington's *WETA Magazine*, the program guide for the capital's public broadcasting station.

Later the museum invited me to participate in a panel discussion to be held in Washington on November 8, 1988, to commemorate the fiftieth anniversary of Kristallnacht. As the final arrangements for the China trip were being made, it turned out that the Washington commemoration was planned for the day after my scheduled return from Shanghai. In preparing for both of these events, I was flooded by recollections of not just our life in Shanghai but also my childhood in Berlin, which had been dormant for a long time. Even though I had dealt with disturbing recollections from my past during psychoanalysis, it was unsettling to suddenly be swept by lifelike images dating back almost half a century. Memories of my parents came to mind frequently and unexpectedly, even though they had died almost two decades earlier, as did surprisingly intense images of my childhood in Berlin.

People from the museum informed me that I would meet the German ambassador to the United States at the Kristallnacht commemoration. The prospect of that meeting brought back my frightened reactions at unexpectedly running into prominent German officials when we visited my mother after her gallbladder surgery in 1937. I recalled feeling enormous relief then when we left the hospital's waiting room for my mother's bedside. Many years later, during my analysis in New York, I realized the intensity of my fears during those hospital visits. My analyst pointed out that the memories of actually being in my mother's room were highly suspect since, as a child approaching five, I would probably not have been allowed to make a bedside visit after what was then major surgery. Apparently, the presence of the Nazi top brass was so frightening that I imagined escaping into my mother's room rather than remain terror struck in the waiting area. In analysis I clearly recalled the German officers' loud *"Heils,"* the crack of their clicking heels, the boots polished to a steely luster, and their uniforms bristling with decorations and holstered pistols.

The recurring memories gave a deeper, often unnerving resonance to the preparations for both my return to Shanghai and my participation in the Kristallnacht panel. I spoke briefly at the panel about my memories of Kristallnacht and many people in the audience seemed affected by my comments. Later, at a reception, the German ambassador introduced himself to me, also indicating that he was moved. I shook his hand, saying, "I am glad to see you at this occasion."

These events reinforced my feelings that the memories of Berlin and Shanghai should be preserved and made the trip to China seem like a return journey into my childhood. I first thought of writing about my childhood memories during a 1985 visit to Germany. I recalled a visit to Schriesheim, a town outside of Heidelberg, where my wife's family had lived until 1938. Lora's family were members of the Jewish community in that town with roots in Schriesheim dating back almost three hundred years. We met with the Rufers, a family that had helped my wife and her parents during the rise of Hitler in the mid-1930s. We were talking about the Jewish community in Schriesheim when the

Rufers' oldest daughter, Annegret, shocked us unintentionally by saying, "I never knew that Jews lived in Schriesheim."

I also remembered a conversation Lora and I had had with some German tourists while on vacation in Norway. On several prior trips to Europe we had decided to speak German only to people who seemed younger than we were. Then, we did not have to wonder about what these people had done either before or during the war, nor would we have to deal with offensive justifications declaring that only a handful of people knew anything at all about the Holocaust. While on a boat trip across a Norwegian fjord we were having a pleasant conversation with a young German couple. Suddenly the young man turned to me and asked, "Your German is so good, why did you ever leave?"

I was stunned by the question and could only say, "You must be joking."

The young man looked at me intently for a moment, flushed, and looked away. "Those were evil times," he said softly. Later, I wished that I had had the presence of mind to have responded that "times" are neutral, it is people who make them evil.

These incidents convinced me that it was important to bear witness to the past. I had resisted previous suggestions to write about my memories because I have neither the training nor the inclination for historical research. My academic and scholarly commitments had always made it difficult to find the time to begin such a major undertaking. Fortunately, the four weeks in China made it possible to refresh my memories. Since the English-language newspaper available in Shanghai was quite skimpy, and there were no foreign-language radio or television broadcasts, the four weeks in China gave me the time to take some notes and begin drafting this personal history.

14 Return to Shanghai

We had never seen the airport while living in Shanghai, but even if we had I would still have been unprepared for the scene facing me when the plane touched down on the runway. Four China Airlines Boeing 747s were parked on the tarmac as we pulled up to a new terminal building. After stepping out of the plane onto a portable staircase, I was immediately struck by two familiar sensations: the intense humidity and the unmistakable smell. Apparently, human waste was still used as fertilizer in China. I reminded myself to avoid eating raw vegetables and most fruits.

A small group from the Shanghai Institute of Education led by Shu Yun-xiang, a specialist in educational evaluation, welcomed me back to China. I had spoken with Shu on the phone while making the final arrangements for the trip and, since his English was clearly just as good as I thought it was from our prior contacts, I was pleased to hear that he would interpret for me during my stay. A waiting institute car took us to my assigned lodging in the guest house of the Shanghai Conservatory of Music, located directly across the street from the Institute of Education.

My room at the guest house had obviously seen grander days. An impressive art deco lighting fixture illuminated some peeling wallpaper in a room with other tell-tale signs of generations of use. It was furnished shabbily but had a large radiator, a color television set, a small refrigerator, an air conditioner connected to exposed wiring, and a telephone. A large thermos of boiled drinking water, with two additional ones in the bathroom, was on top of the refrigerator. No amount of cleaning could remove the stains left on the fixtures in the adjoining private bathroom by years of intense use. Basins had been strategically placed under bathroom plumbing and fixtures to catch water leaks. Some newer pipes replaced dilapidated plastic tubing that had not been removed when the newer fixtures were installed.

In my mind's eye I compared the room's shabby furnishings with the contents of the single rooms in which my parents and I had lived in Shanghai. Our homes then were only a little larger than my room in the guest house, and the quality of the furniture in the rooms was comparable. Back then, however, we had no desk, no central heating, no private bathroom, no running water for our toilets, no hot water, no telephone, no refrigeration other than a small icebox, no air conditioning—not even a fan—and of course no television.

Shu was looking at me expectantly, and I realized that he must have asked me something that had not registered through the forty years my mind was traveling. "I'm sorry Mr. Shu, I didn't quite hear you. Could you say that again please?"

"This," Shu said, pointing to the room and furnishings, "must be primitive by your standards."

"You know, I have two sets of standards, and this compares very favorably to what we had when I lived in Shanghai." I was glad to see Shu smile appreciatively. My answer must really have pleased him, since I could make out just enough Chinese to realize that he repeated it two days later during our meeting with the president and deans of the Shanghai Institute of Education, who also seemed to like my response.

Before leaving my hosts informed me about the arrangements for meals in the dining room. While unpacking, I was amused to realize that tomorrow's breakfast in the conservatory would mark the first Chinese meal I ever had in Shanghai. During our decade in China we ate only kosher food and, therefore, never ate in any native restaurants. Even though I have Chinese food quite regularly now, my fondness for that cuisine was acquired entirely in the United States.

An older Chinese man who was the attendant on my floor of the guest house brought the *China Daily*, an English-language newspaper, and while showing me how to use the hand-held shower motioned for me to ignore the obsolete plumbing fixtures. After he left I was startled by a cockroach slithering across the floor. Indeed, I had returned to Shanghai. I suddenly also realized that the attendant had left the bathtub filled with continuously running cold water to discourage roaches and other bugs.

Getting ready for breakfast the following morning reminded me of just how uncomfortable even the most routine daily tasks still were in Shanghai. While filling a glass with water to brush my teeth, I remembered that it was dangerous even to rinse my mouth with tap water, much less to drink it. The heavily polluted Yangtze River is the main source of Shanghai's water supply, and even boiled water has the unmistakable taste left by massive additions of chlorine that, nevertheless, failed to make the water safe for drinking. I filled a glass from the thermos only to find that it was boiling hot. On succeeding days I poured the water shortly after waking so that it was lukewarm by the time it was needed. I made a mental note to buy some bottled mineral water, which would not have to be boiled.

During breakfast I learned that my impression that the guest house must have been an imposing institution at one time was correct, since the building was formerly the Belgian consulate. Of course, we came to Shanghai originally as a result of my father's failed attempt to cross into Belgium. If he had succeeded in getting to Antwerp safely, or if our family had remained in Berlin, we would not have survived the Holocaust. Most Belgian Jews, and virtually all the Jews living in Germany, were exterminated in the concentration camps.

My schedule on the first day back in Shanghai was left open so that I could rest up from the long trip. Shu used the free time to show me around the campus of the Shanghai Institute of Education and the surrounding area. The institute's auditorium, a building with a large hall that could seat up to a thousand people, seemed familiar to me. Indeed, it should have been familiar because I was startled to recognize that it had formerly been the new synagogue, attended mainly by the Russian Jewish community while I lived in Shanghai. It took me a while to identify the former synagogue because all the street names had been changed. The synagogue had been completed in 1941 and used to be located on Rue Tenant de la Tour; the street was now called Xian Yang Nan Lu.

The synagogue was located quite a distance away from our homes in Hongkew; therefore I attended services there on only a few occasions during my last year in Shanghai while working in the store on Avenue Joffre. The outer walls of the former synagogue seemed darker than I remembered them. The synagogue used to have a light stucco facade which—like other buildings in the area—had turned a dingy dark gray from years of air pollution. Even though I am no longer very observant of religious rituals, I felt an urge to put on the customary head covering required in synagogues while touring the building, despite the fact that we could not find a foundation stone or any other marks to indicate that this had ever been a house of worship.

During a meeting with Professor Jia-xiang Zhang, president of the Institute of Education, and some of his deans and senior administrators on my second day in Shanghai, I mentioned, with the help of Shu's translation, that I was familiar with the institute's auditorium. Zhang nodded and said that the institute had been using the synagogue because there were no more Jews living in the city. "We will be happy to give it back to the Jewish community," the president said, "when they return to Shanghai."

The Conservatory of Music, in whose guest house I was staying, was located on Fen Yang Lu, a block away from the former synagogue.

I was startled again when someone mentioned that the conservatory was formerly the luxurious French Club located on the street I had known as Rue Pichon. The surgery on my neck had been performed at the Shanghai Jewish Hospital located on Rue Pichon. In response to my questions, Shu said that there was a hospital specializing in the treatment of ear, nose, and throat conditions located about a block and a half away from the conservatory. We walked to the Shanghai Otolaryngological Hospital, and I immediately recognized it. The hospital's main waiting room appeared largely unchanged, except that it now urgently needed a new coat of paint.

There were many differences between contemporary Shanghai and the city I remembered. The Institute of Education faces Huai Hai Lu, formerly Avenue Joffre, but still a main street and every bit as crowded now as it was when we lived there. Under French sovereignty the clashing metal wheels of trolley cars against metal tracks on Avenue Joffre created quite a din augmented by the incessant ringing of the tram's bell by conductors warning other traffic to get out of the way. The trolleys used to have two cars and three classes. In present-day Shanghai, both on Huai Hai Lu and on all other major streets, quiet electrically powered buses, attached to overhead wiring, provided the predominant form of public transportation. The electric buses were even more jammed than the trolleys had been forty years ago and also had two compartments, attached by a flexible connection, though they were all of one class.

Surprisingly, such egalitarianism is not universal in contemporary China. While visiting Soochow, a city well known for its gardens, we took our meals in the staff dining room at Soochow University. During lunch I noticed that a special table had been set in one corner of the dining room, separated from the rest of the hall by screens. Attendants hovered near that table at all times and served each of the people there individually, in contrast to the family style service in the rest of the dining room. I assumed that the senior administrators of the university were being honored with such special service, but was informed that the table was reserved for members of the Communist party committee.

One striking difference between the present and past was the absence of rickshaws and the virtual disappearance of pedicabs—a vehicle much like a tricycle with a carriage for one or two passengers in the rear—propelled by a man pedaling the vehicle from the front. Occasionally, workers could be seen using a bicycle to tow a cart bearing heavy loads. It became clear that for people engaged in physical labor work was as brutally demanding as it always had been in China.

I remembered the stark contrasts in Chinese people's clothing when we lived in Shanghai. Many exquisite women wearing elegantly ornate silk shifts could be seen in downtown Shanghai, side by side with others wearing simple cotton peasant pants and tunics; the poorest people often wore threadbare clothes or rags. Nowadays, there were fewer extremes in people's attire, and garments quite similar to the informal clothes of young people throughout the Western world were the rule. I was told that traditional Chinese attire had virtually disappeared, since it is difficult to do factory or office work while wearing the traditional garments.

Now most of Shanghai's older buildings gave an impression of grim shabbiness from years of use by a population much larger than originally anticipated. It did not help much to see laundry drying on what used to be elegant verandahs in the former French concession. Another surprising sight was the occasional stovepipe jutting out of windows that were graceful living rooms forty years ago; evidently people had to rely on coal stoves during the winter, much the way we used to in Hongkew. I guessed that the maintenance of the residential heating systems, even in this formerly elegant section of the city, had been about as effective as that of the water pipes in the conservatory's guest house. Private homes seemed to be in even poorer shape than governmental and institutional structures, while hotels catering to tourists seemed to be the best maintained structures.

Tourists staying in clean hotels, air conditioned in the summer and well heated in the winter, are relatively insulated from the difficulties of the average Chinese person's daily life. During sightseeing trips they get little impression of the primitive facilities available to the Chinese people—until they have to use the toilets. The lavatories, whether in the school where I lectured or in places that we visited, were invariably filthy, they rarely contained toilet paper, and their stench was reminiscent of the smelly toilet buckets we had used during the war. Of course, the facilities in most Chinese one-room homes are even more primitive, since there are few toilets with running water. Even modern apartment buildings in China usually have no hot water unless it is heated on a stove, and in most houses running water is generally available only at one faucet shared by all the residents.

Foreign visitors staying at the guest house warned me not to be surprised if my hosts were fairly distant about contacts outside of their official responsibilities. Apparently, the friendliness seen in work-related settings with Chinese people is often replaced by hesitation about social meetings stemming from an official policy of discouraging close contact with foreigners. Foreign students at the conservatory told me that it was apparently official policy to keep them apart from their Chinese colleagues. The foreigners lived on dorm floors that housed no Chinese students and had to use a different staircase than the Chinese students. The floors on which the Chinese students lived were closed to foreign students. Several foreigners spoke Chinese fluently, some had studied in Shanghai for over two years, yet none knew the full name of even a single Chinese student.

Some foreigners also felt they were under discreet surveillance. Toward the end of my return to Shanghai I once asked a young foreign student to my room to translate some papers dealing with the trip. The woman asked me to keep my door ajar. When I reacted to her request with amused surprise she said, "Oh no, it isn't what you think at all." She motioned to the attendant on the floor; I had seen him peeking at us when we walked up the stairs. Once we arrived at my room the attendant suddenly found a variety of reasons for flitting back and forth in the corridor in front of the room. "He is going to report my visit, and I didn't want them to get the wrong idea or be seen in a suspicious light."

During my stay I learned that life in China is difficult for academics, scientists, and similar professionals. After Lora joined me for a week's stay we invited two young faculty members from the Shanghai Institute of Education to dinner one evening in a good, though by no means luxurious, restaurant. The bill for our party almost equaled six weeks' salary for these faculty members. Paradoxically enough, life is much better for peasants and laborers, who could supplement their usual wages by doing additional work for extra pay. But teachers, professors, and other professionals had little opportunity for extra income and seemed to have a life of none too genteel poverty.

We met many scientists and professional people who were eager to update their knowledge and skills, often at considerable personal inconvenience. I was struck by that even before my arrival in China. On the flight from Tokyo to Shanghai a Chinese physicist was seated next to me. He was returning home after spending four years at a scientific institute in the United States. During his entire stay his only contact with the family he had left behind was through the mail. He could not afford even a single trip home, and neither the research institutes in Beijing and the United States nor the Chinese government would help him defray the costs. Naturally, he was eagerly anticipating the reunion with his wife and children—a son who was eleven when he left for America and had now reached his fifteenth birthday and a daughter who was then nine years old and now thirteen. In view of the long separation from his family I was curious to know if my neighbor thought that his stay in the United Sates had been worthwhile. "Oh, of course," he answered with some surprise at the question, "I learned so much."

Despite being distrusted by the government and their relatively low financial status it was clear that academics were respected by the people. We experienced an amusing sidelight to the respect in which professors were held. My task at the Shanghai Institute of Education, a training institution for secondary school teachers and administrators, was to lecture about recent developments in human learning and instruction to a group of eighty-five secondary school principals and vice principals. I failed to generate much discussion during my two-and-a-half-hour lectures at the institute, nor could I stimulate many questions. I attributed the reticence to the novelty of the subject matter to the audience, but was surprised and somewhat envious when my wife delivered a part of one of my lectures and received lots of questions and discussion. Lora, a reading specialist, described the reading program in her New York school district. I asked Shu why the principals questioned Lora so readily, yet were reluctant to raise any questions with me. He pointed out that Lora was a teacher and as principals they were accustomed to questioning teachers. However, they thought it might be disrespectful to question a professor.

Welcome sign during one of our school visits in Shanghai, 1988. (Author's collection)

Shu Yun-xiang, my interpreter, and I in front of the Shanghai Institute of Education. (Author's collection)

Shu Yun-xiang interpreting my lectures to the principals at the Shanghai Institute of Education. (Author's collection)

Lora Tobias lecturing to the principals at the Shanghai Institute of Education. (Author's collection)

Motorized junks in Soochow Creek. (Author's collection)

Stalls on Chusan Road in Hongkew. (Author's collection)

Residents of house 16 in the 315 Wayside Road lane in 1988. (Author's collection)

Residents of our room in house 16 in the 315 Wayside Road lane in 1988. (Author's collection)

15 Back in Hongkew

*D*uring one week of my stay Shu arranged for us to have the institute's car for a visit to Hongkew, now called Hongkow. As we drove over the bridge across the Soochow Creek Lora and I got out of the car to look around. The creek seemed to be about as dirty as it had always been and Shu confirmed that water pollution was still a huge problem. I also noticed that there were just as many junks in the creek as I remembered, except that now many of them were motorized.

We drove along Broadway, now called Dongdaming Lu. Freighters from different countries could still be seen at the docks parallel to Broadway but we saw no passenger liners. The many stores on Broadway that used to be bars and houses of prostitution had apparently disappeared. I also did not see any prostitutes cruising along the streets, nor was there any sign of the multitudes of beggars who used to camp out on Broadway.

Even though I had forgotten the number of our house in the 737 Lane of Broadway, my steps unhesitatingly took me to number 21. Some present-day residents were lounging in front of our old house and looked at me with curious expressions that turned dubious when Shu explained that I used to live there. I guessed that they must have been surprised that foreigners ever lived here, in one of the poorer areas of the city. A large department store had replaced the textile warehouse that had been next door. I asked Shu to inquire about what had happened to the warehouse. The residents seemed surprised that I knew of the warehouse and said that it had been replaced by the department store some years ago. After that they finally appeared convinced that I had actually lived there, telling Shu that I had an excellent memory. Since we were not invited inside, I was content to wander about the lane. All the houses were now shabbier and more dilapidated than I had remembered them being forty years earlier, but the lane was otherwise unchanged.

We then drove to the house on Wayside Road, now Changyang Lu, inside the former ghetto where we lived throughout the war. I was surprised to see a new eighteen-story tower under construction at the intersection of the former Wayside Road and Broadway and was informed that it was supposed to become a new hotel. A new pedestrian walkway was at the corner opposite the future hotel to prevent gridlock among the oceans of bicycles, other vehicles, and pedestrians. With these exceptions, the neighborhood was pretty much the way it had been when we lived there.

The massive five-story building that had housed the U.S. army repatriation center after the war was still across the street from the 315 Wayside Road lane. I recalled that the building had been constructed of very light bricks; now it had turned a dingy gray and was occupied by different manufacturing concerns. The shop that used to sell boiled water near our lane no longer existed, though Shu told us that there still were such stores in other parts of Shanghai. The few remaining water stores had been modernized and the ladles had been replaced by spigots at the base of the water tanks.

Unlike the residents at our former home on Broadway, the present residents of house 16 in the lane knew that foreigners had once lived there. When we approached the house a retired couple living in the room once occupied by the Attermans invited us into the house and then insisted that we have some coffee. They mentioned that Rita Feder, formerly Atterman, had visited a year or two earlier. They proudly showed off their prize possession, a portable washing machine that had to be wheeled over to the common water spout when ready for a wash. My wife asked if they had ever thought of doing some of the neighbors' laundry for a fee, and they seemed intrigued by the idea.

We then went upstairs to see the room in which my parents and I had lived. The room had been shortened by two or three feet, and that space had been added to the small chamber formerly occupied by the two Mirrer Yeshiva students. A solid wall reaching all the way up to the ceiling had replaced the plywood separator. A young couple now lived in our former room. When word of our visit circulated in the house, many of the residents came in to meet us and gladly posed for a group picture with us in the lane in front of the house.

We also noticed that the collection of human waste had been modernized. Residents now emptied their slop buckets at a central area in each lane; these were eventually pumped out by motorized vehicles, quite similar to tanker trucks bringing gasoline to service stations, equipped with heavy hoses to empty the waste receptacles. I remembered how unpleasant it had been for the residents to take turns letting the Chinese workers into the house before dawn each morning to empty the slop buckets into wheelbarrows. However, the foul odor lingering in the lane now after the trucks had picked up the waste was identical to that left by the wheelbarrows.

I was especially moved when we reached the two connected buildings further up on Wayside Road that used to house the Mirrer Yeshiva. In the intervening years I had learned a good deal more about Chiune Sugihara, the Japanese consul-general in Kovno whose heroism had made it possible for the yeshiva to flee from Europe. David Kranzler tells the story in *Japanese, Nazis, and Jews: The Jewish Refugee Community of Shanghai, 1938–1945*, and there have also been a number of references to it in the media. When Sugihara was overwhelmed with refugees pleading for visas, he asked his government for permission to issue transit visas to the refugees on three different occasions, but was refused each time. Before the war Britain had urged the Japanese to turn the refugees away, warning that the Jews would become a burden to Japan. Despite all of that, Sugihara was unable to turn his back on the Jews clamoring at the gates of the Japanese consulate and followed his own conscience by issuing the transit visas to the refugees, defying orders from his government.

Sugihara was eventually removed from his post in Kovno and assigned to other positions during World War II. When he finally returned to Japan in 1947 he was forced to resign from the foreign service in disgrace. In 1984 Yad Vashem, the Holocaust museum in Jerusalem, bestowed on Sugihara the title "righteous among the nations," an honor shared by such heroic figures as Oscar Schindler and Raoul Wallenberg. Without Sugihara's help, the last 1,200 refugees to arrive in Shanghai, including the entire membership of the Mirrer Yeshiva, would certainly not have survived. The Jews remaining in Kovno when the Germans captured the city were either shot immediately, died in the ghettos, or were exterminated in the concentration camps.

The buildings formerly occupied by the Mirrer Yeshiva seemed to be in somewhat worse shape now than the houses in our old lane; many windows had shattered glass panes and there was little evidence of recent repair. The former yeshiva was part of a group of buildings that used to be among the nicer ones on Wayside Road; these structures were three stories high, compared with the two stories typical in Hongkew.

Chusan Road, which had been the center of refugee life in Hongkew and used to have many refugee-owned businesses and some European style coffeehouses, was still a bustling place. The tiny grass plots formerly in front of each house on the street and the coffeehouses had disappeared. Stalls selling clothing, textiles, and decorations had been built over the former grass plots all along the street, but the street was still a beehive of activity. The huge jail on Ward Road seemed unchanged.

Oihel Moshe, where my bar mitzvah was celebrated in 1945, was now a psychiatric hospital. (More recent visitors have informed me that the former synagogue is now a museum commemorating the refugees' stay in Shanghai.) When we walked into the courtyard in front of the building a Chinese man told us that we could not enter the hospital. I asked to see the hospital's director and gave him my card, identifying me as a professor at the City College of New York. I told the director, with Shu acting as interpreter, that I was a psychologist and had interned in several psychiatric facilities; thus nothing I would see would surprise me. However, I made it clear that this was an entirely personal visit, not a professional one, and that I had celebrated my bar mitzvah in the former synagogue. The director immediately gave us the run of the place and accompanied us on a tour of the facility.

The former synagogue now housed patients in the acute intensive phase of psychotic episodes. Patients who did not improve after three months were transferred to another facility for long-term treatment. The former main synagogue auditorium, where my father and the other men used to have their seats, was now a recreation area for the staff. The bima, a raised podium where the cantor once stood and from where I had read from the Torah scrolls on my bar mitzvah, had disappeared. The verandah on the second floor, where the women used to worship, had been eliminated and now consisted of different offices. The third floor, which used to house the Talmud Torah, was now occupied by wards for female patients. The women seemed to be heavily sedated and did not take any notice of our visit as they shambled along drowsily in their own world. The former matzo bakery, in back of the synagogue, now housed the men's wards. In contrast to the women, the men seemed quite alert and waved to us, asking if we had any American cigarettes.

The police station where Ghoya had lorded it over the refugees was located half a block away from the synagogue. It also seemed largely unchanged, as was the rest of Hongkew. The three movie theaters inside the boundaries of the former ghetto were still being used except that they now showed only Chinese films. A few blocks away from Oihel Moshe was the Eastern Theater, where we had seen many American movies after the war. I remembered that most of the spoken dialogue had often been unintelligible; we never knew whether that was caused by films of poor quality or by ancient equipment. Shu arranged for me to wander into the theater; the sound seemed clearer, but since the characters spoke only in Chinese it was still unintelligible to me.

On the way back to the guest house we stopped at an elementary school a block away from Soochow Creek. One of the people in the group to whom I was lecturing was the principal there and had invited us to visit. After watching a math lesson, we gathered in the obligatory meeting attended by the teacher we had observed, the principal, and the vice principals. We enjoyed some tea and talked about the lesson, the school, and the students. Before we left I asked Shu to tell the principal, "If my life had turned out differently, I could well have been one of your students." I was glad to see that she was pleased by that thought.

We were invited to many schools during our visit and observed a number of excellent English lessons. At the meetings after the lessons we were astounded to find that the teachers invariably could not understand us, even though we were careful to speak simply and slowly, nor were they able to speak any English spontaneously. Apparently the lessons we had watched were so carefully scripted and so frequently practiced that the teachers appeared reasonably fluent, but neither the teachers nor their students could speak the language easily in casual encounters. While the government makes a considerable effort to teach English, both in the schools and over television, few Chinese people have an easy facility with the spoken language. We were sometimes approached on the street by total strangers who wanted to practice speaking English. In Beijing a gentleman accompanied us and our interpreter for over half the day merely to practice his correct and formal English.

The most frequently heard English words in China were "Change money?" Much to the annoyance of our interpreter, we were often approached about changing money, especially in areas frequented by tourists. As was the case during the time I lived in Shanghai, black market exchange rates were substantially higher than those offered at banks, but most foreigners were rightfully afraid to transact any business on the street. A young American couple staying at the conservatory guest house did follow one of the money changers to a back alley to exchange one hundred U.S. dollars. Since such transactions were illegal, the money changer surreptitiously and rapidly counted out the Chinese currency before disappearing. When the Americans returned to the guest house they found that they had been given only about sixty percent of the Chinese money they had expected for the one hundred dollars.

The president of the Shanghai Institute of Education gave a banquet in my honor attended by all the deans, other administrators, and the chancellor of Shanghai's public school system, whom I had met when he traveled to New York a year earlier. When I mentioned my visits to Hongkew and other places that had been significant in the life of the Jewish community, the chancellor told me that his main office was formerly the Shanghai Jewish School, which had been attended by children of the Sephardic and Russian Jews, and by children of some of the more affluent refugees. The building that housed the Kadoorie school had apparently been torn down and replaced by a factory. I had learned before my visit that the three cemeteries filled by refugees who had died during our stay in China had been bulldozed during the Cultural Revolution and that factory buildings had been constructed on those sites. I did not mention the cemeteries during my return visit.

We were struck by the fact that none of the schools we visited, and very few private residences, had central heating or other means of providing warmth in the winter. While the temperatures were mild during the late autumn weeks of the trip, I recalled that the high humidity and gales coming from the north made for some pretty frigid winters. Apparently the people's major defense against the cold is to wear the same tufted garments we Europeans were so dubious about during the war.

We were frequently asked to give our impression of Chinese education, and I remember especially being questioned about that by a journalist interviewing me for an educational publication. Being aware of Chinese sensitivity to criticism, I prefaced my comments by describing how impressive the students, staff, and facilities were. I also mentioned the formidable achievement of instituting at least nine years of mandatory education since I had lived in Shanghai. My interviewer realized that I was trying to avoid sounding critical and said, "You know, we are not afraid of criticism."

I laughed. "After living here for so many years, I'm not so sure of that. But as a friend of China I want to make helpful suggestions, rather than criticisms." I indicated that we had seen many impressive lessons and had the feeling that the schools often placed a heavy emphasis on remembering. It might be useful, I suggested, to concentrate more on problem solving and application of what was learned, and less on rote learning. The reporter, and others who asked about our impressions of Chinese education, generally agreed with these comments.

During my last walk through Hongkew before returning to the United States I was busy recording some of the places that had special meaning to me with our video camera, while my wife was taking photos with her 35-millimeter camera. A Chinese man working at a fruit stand asked Shu why we were taking so many photos of this area. When we explained that I had lived here forty years ago, the man said, "Things haven't changed much, have they?"

Epilogue

I usually briefed Shu by giving him an outline of the contents of my lectures to the principals a few days in advance so that he could prepare himself and look up technical words that might be difficult to translate on the spot. At the end of my last lecture I added a written personal note that I gave to Shu for translation.

> I am happy to have been welcomed so warmly in today's Shanghai, much the way about sixteen thousand other Jews were welcomed here almost fifty years ago. Had we not found safe haven in China then, most of us would not have survived, the way six million of our relatives, friends, and other members of our people were killed during the Second World War. Even though our life here during the Second World War was not easy, we realized how lucky we were to have found shelter in Shanghai when we heard about the Auschwitz, Belsen, and Treblinka concentration camps. I am grateful to the Chinese people for letting us live among them peacefully during that terrible time, and am happy to have been able to return.

I was aware of being deeply moved while making these personal comments, though I was surprised to hear my voice crack at the mention of the concentration camps. I am just as moved by the memory of that event today.

Index

SIGMUND TOBIAS has served as the president of the
Division of Educational Psychology of the American Psychological
Association, was editor of *Instructional Science: An International Journal
of Learning and Cognition,* and is coeditor (with Dexter Fletcher) of
Training Handbook, sponsored by the Division of Educational
Psychology of the American Psychological Association. He spent
many years at the City University of New York and is
currently a Distinguished Scholar in the educational psychology
program at Fordham University.

MICHAEL BERENBAUM is president and CEO of the
Survivors of the Shoah Visual History Foundation. He was project
director of the United States Holocaust Memorial Museum and
later served as director of its Research Institute. He is the author
of twelve books, including *The World Must Know* and *After Tragedy and
Triumph.*